Fullness of Time by Ray Harris is a creative collection prayers, poetry, anecdotes, and art. It beautifully reflects the author's ministry as Spiritual Care Coordinator at Tabor Village, Abbotsford, B.C, where he regularly led morning prayers, offered meditations on Scripture, and provided spiritual care to the senior residents. His compassionate care and creativity are evident throughout the book, and I especially appreciate the stories he shares of his interactions with various residents--singing and praying with them, sharing a laugh, offering words of kindness, and simply being present. The book includes both an index to Scripture, as well as an index to various topics like change, growth, death, and eternity. If you're interested in devotional reading especially for seniors, if you're a pastor or chaplain looking for a resource of short meditations, I recommend *Fullness of Time.*

April Yamasaki,
Writer, Editor, Speaker - author of *Four Gifts, Sacred Pauses,* and *On the Way With Jesus* - https://aprilyamasaki.comWhen You Work for the Church: https://whenyouworkforthechurch.com
Facebook: https://www.facebook.com/april.yamasaki
Twitter: @SacredPauses

Ray Harris has put together an invaluable collection of personal experiences and scriptural insights with a deep understanding of the human heart. These devotionals should have a universal appeal, reflecting an appreciation of God's Spirit at work in every heart. Over the period of his ministry at Tabor, Ray has touched many lives and this devotional should allow his ministry to extend even further. I can well identify with the experiences of senior's home ministry shown in his anecdotes. I appreciate the love and affection his stories show as he navigates the challenges and communicates the joys of chaplaincy. The daily readings should be equally valuable for personal devotions and as an outline for ministry in a wide variety of contexts. I look forward to utilizing this great resource!

Chris Thoutenhoofd,
Chaplain, Tabor Village, Abbotsford, B.C.

Ray has used his life and ministry insights to lead older adults in a time of reflection and response on the Word of God. The devotionals, poems and pictures all speak to the seasons of life with an assurance of God's faithful presence. I can confidently endorse *The Fullness of Time* as a book of devotionals that will lead older adults to journey through the seasons of life with an assurance of God's presence. In this book, individuals will be encouraged by Scripture as they are guided to reflect and respond on a personal level. I would also recommend this book as a resource that the Christian Chaplain could use in offering spiritual care to others addressing the challenges of life, relationships, and faith. This is a book filled with peace and renewal.

Gloria J. Woodland, DMin.
Chaplaincy Program Director
ACTS Seminaries | Trinity Western University
Associate Professor of Chaplaincy Studies & Spiritual Care
MB Seminary National Seminary of the MB Churches of Canada

Ray Harris' new devotional is designed as a weekly lectionary, taking us alphabetically through the books of Scripture, through Lent, Advent, and Ordinary Time. Far from rigidly structured, however, the book follows a gracious arc, and an arc of Grace. Harris offers us thoughts and experiences gleaned from his time as chaplain at Tabor Village. A book of words and silences, of meditation.

Robert Martens,
writer, editor, poet.

Fullness of Time

Devotionals, Poems, Pictures, and Prayers

Ray Harris

Bev,

It has been a privilege
to serve your parents at Tabor
Blessings to you,
Ray Harris

Mill Lake Books

1.	Christian spirituality 2. Bible 3. Devotional 4. Poetry 5. Chaplaincy 6. Spirituality for older adults 7. Prayer

All Scripture quotations unless otherwise indicated, are taken from the Holy Bible, New International Version NIV, copyright 1978, 1984.

Harris, Raymond Stanley, 1956-

Published by Mill Lake Books
Chilliwack, BC
Canada
jamescoggins.wordpress.com/mill-lake-books

Book layout and design by Lyra Dyck
Cover photography by Amy Bergen

Printed by Lightning Source, distributed by Ingram

Special thanks to Hildegarde Bandsmer, Jennifer Klassen, Robert Dent, and Robert Martens for reading and editing the manuscript.

ISBN: 978-1-998787-05-0

TABLE OF CONTENTS

INTRODUCTION

Measuring time is helpful for humans. We sometimes talk about "time management," by which we really mean managing ourselves within time, striving to make the most of every opportunity in our lives. We can't manage time.

We employ many different methods to measure time: calendars, clocks, computers, and constellations. Time is enjoyed in the seasons of life, in the beauty of nature, in getting to know God, and in developing deep human relationships.

During my time as Spiritual Care Coordinator at Tabor Village, Abbotsford, BC, I had the privilege of leading morning prayers. Over my four years this looked different from season to season, but generally fifty to sixty residents attended, listening, praying, singing, in three locations: The Living Room and Willow Dining Room at Tabor, and Valhaven Home. Each session included biblical meditations.

I was encouraged to collect some of these devotional meditations to share with others beyond the Tabor campus. The devotionals in this book reflect the precious privilege of sharing meaningful time with these older adults on their journey in their present season of life. I based these Tabor Morning Prayers on an alphabetical walk through all sixty-six books of the Bible, over a period of forty months.

The structure of this book follows the yearly journey through the seasons winter, spring, summer, and fall, and allows the Church Calendar to inspire and inform the poems, pictures and reflections. Each week includes three devotionals, a poem, prayers, pictures, affirmations, and anecdotes. The poems reflect various seasons and spiritual impressions I have written over several years. The weekly affirmations are my humble *Pensées*, thoughts, or aphorisms which I hope will encourage and be thought-provoking. The pictures are by family, friends, and Tabor tenants. Most of the photographs are of the Fraser Valley, in order to celebrate a sense of place and beauty. The anecdotes are true stories of conversations and experiences in Tabor Village. Some stories are extended or embellished, but they recall actual events; however, all the names have been changed to provide respect and anonymity for these lovely individuals, many of whom are now passed through the veil. Each day, each month, each season has joys and challenges.

Time is a gift. There is a fullness of time. It's about time: Church year, Julian Calendar, ordered time for a heart of wisdom.

It's time.

WINTER

December – February

Advent of Presence

The story is old
      But it's still Good News!
      Nova! Nova! First Noel
      Told every year, gospel, the good story.
A deep inner joy; founded on hope
Found in that boy
Taking on flesh while retaining deity.
Humble freshness, incarnate dignity.
      So, you see
      Old news is good news
      Round and around
      Covering cosmos
      Treading new ground.
Cousin John from upcountry
Prophetic and bold; challenging attitudes
Wilderness scold!
Preparing the way, the Herald of Joy
Not based on circumstance
Or prepackaged ploy.
Advent of Presence
No foe can destroy.

Meditation - New Things

☀ **Praying Psalm 1:** Lord, allow me to embrace the joys of positively delighting in you. May I flourish and bear fruit. Thank you, God, for watching over me.

📖 **Scripture Text** - Acts 2:1-13
Amazed and perplexed, they asked one another, "What does this mean?" Acts 2:12

God delights in doing new things. As we start a new year, we look ahead with anticipation to what God wants to do in our lives, in our communities, and in our world. God was doing a new thing in the creation of the church recorded in Acts 2. It caused amazement, confusion, and questions. As we look to the year ahead, perhaps there will be seasons of challenge; certainly there will be times of opportunity, and excitement. The Spirit wants to do new things in our lives today and in the year ahead. Jesus is the head of the church and each of us as followers of Jesus are parts of the body. This assures us of two things as we enter this New Year: Jesus will lead us as we follow, and secondly, we do not walk alone – we have brothers and sisters in Christ to walk this journey with us. Be encouraged, amazed and maybe even perplexed by the new things God is doing.

🎵 **Suggested Song:** "Great is Thy Faithfulness"

🙏 **Pray:** Heavenly Father, thank you for the new things you are doing in my life. Open my eyes and ears so that I may see you more clearly, that I may follow Jesus more closely, and that I may rely on the Holy Spirit to lead, guide, and encourage me throughout this year. In Jesus' name, Amen.

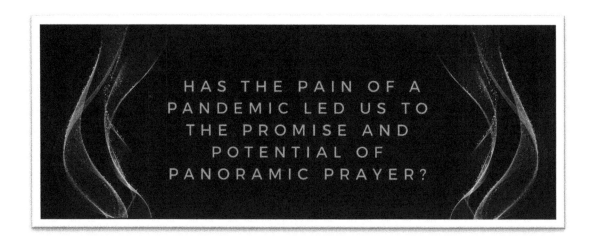

HAS THE PAIN OF A PANDEMIC LED US TO THE PROMISE AND POTENTIAL OF PANORAMIC PRAYER?

Meditation - Turn Around

Praying Psalm 2: Lord, in the anger, turmoil, evil and trouble of our world, may I hear your laughter. Thank you for placing leaders where you want them. Grant wisdom, humility, and submission.

Scripture Text - Acts 2:37-41
Repent and be baptized everyone of you, in the name of Jesus Christ for the forgiveness of your sins. Acts 2:38

Most of us like to walk and enjoy the fresh air. Sometimes that means having the assistance of someone to help us, if we are in a wheelchair or using a walker. But there are times when we are on our walk when we get disoriented, we lose our way, and we need to seek directions. Sometimes the way forward requires us to stop, turn around, and find our way. The word *repent* means to turn around. When Peter replied to the crowds' question, "What must we do to be saved?" he said, "Turn around and find your way in Jesus Christ." A significant part of God's work in our lives is forgiveness. In the Lord's Prayer we pray regularly, "Forgive us our sins as we forgive those who sin against us." We receive release, freedom, and forgiveness. We see God's forgiveness and enjoy God's promises – promises for us and for our children and for generations to come (verse 39).

Winter Moon, Eleanor

Suggested Song: "Amazing Grace"

Pray: Loving Father, we confess our sins to you again this day. May we also forgive those who have sinned against us. And as we turn around, repent, and face you and your love for us, we ask you to guide us through this day and make us a blessing to others, in Jesus' name. Amen.

Meditation – Devoted

Praying Psalm 3: Loving Father, I seek you and your protection. Shield me from attack, from danger, from enemies. Thank you for your victory and blessings.

Scripture Text - Acts 2:42-47
They devoted themselves to the apostles' teaching and to fellowship, to the breaking of bread and to prayer. Acts 2:42

Every time we gathered for morning prayers at Tabor Home we would spend time in God's word, we would sing songs of our faith, we would apply a passage of scripture to our lives, and we always committed ourselves to praying. The pattern is a very old one. It was modelled for us two thousand years ago by the first community of Jesus' followers. Tabor strives to be a community of prayer. Many of the older adults would ask, "What can I do for God at this stage of my life?" One significant answer is "pray." Our prayer time would focus on our own needs and concerns, we would pray for our families and city, for our province, our country, and the world. Prayer included those who had never heard about the love of God. Today as you devote yourselves to God's word and to service of the community of faith and the wider community through prayer, God will open new doors of understanding and of ways to serve in the Kingdom.

Suggested Song: "Wonderful Words of Life"

Pray: Father, thank you for the Bible. Thank you for the way you speak to us through your Word. Thank you for the example of the early Christians who devoted themselves to spending time in the word, to fellowship, to breaking bread, and to prayer. I want to follow their example today and, in the year, ahead, in Jesus' name, Amen.

The Same Old Songs

"Joy to the World" was playing in the lounge. Gruff Gordon said, "Every year we hear the same old songs – over and over again!" "You don't like Christmas music, Gord?" I asked. Some of us had been discussing the beautiful carols and songs of the season. He hadn't been part of the conversation, so when he chimed in with his question about the same songs every year, I was surprised he had been listening in, and that he had an opinion. We sing the same songs each year because they speak to our hearts.

We Are All In the Pageant

We are all in the Pageant.
Costumes askew, quizzical,
Wondering what to do?
How did I get myself into this?
Like the shepherds
We just try to do our jobs.
Serving some guy,
a farmer or landowner
We may like and know well
    – or not.
Like the angels (really)
no ordinary people,
    no mere mortals but beings of everlasting splendor,
Who also have good news to share.
 Like foreigners seeking
    on a journey,
Give us a chalice for Frankincense
and gumdrops of Myrrh.
 Marred by life's knocks, but
Immured in Love.
Even Mary and Joseph
   are Types for our best acts of surrender
    and simple faith,
Excusable scenes of doubt.
 Hand me that bathrobe,
the halo, or wings,
Deck me in glitter, fine robes,
    costume rings.
 Push me onstage where everyone sees
Grant me deep Joy
    and let my acts please.

Meditation - Faith + Action

☼ **Praying Psalm 4:** Answer me, hear me, have mercy on me, free me. I release my fears, any anger, and my doubts to you, Lord. Thank you for your smile, Lord, your joy, your abundant blessing.

📖 **Scripture Text** - Acts 3:1-10
He jumped to his feet and began to walk. Then he went with them into the temple courts, walking and jumping, and praising God. Acts 3:8

Today's text speaks about a transformative new beginning for a lame man. God was able to meet this person at his point of need, and faith in God, not "silver or gold," resulted in a radical new start. Faith plus action leads us forward. If Peter had not had faith in the name of Jesus, he would never have been able to offer this powerful, life-changing adventure. If the man who received healing did not stand up and walk, he would have remained in his impoverished condition. Do you need a fresh touch of faith in your life today? Where is faith plus action required in our life and the lives of others around us? The result of the new start in this story was that God received praise! (verse 8) Too often our stories begin and end with ourselves. Today's text reminds us that it begins and ends with worshipping God.

🎵 **Suggested Song:** Doxology – "Praise God from Whom All Blessings Flow"

🙏 **Prayer:** Heavenly Father, Jesus taught us that if we have faith the size of a tiny seed, we can do amazing things. Thank you for the example of Peter's bold faith. Give me faith to do the things you call me to. And I will give you all the praise, in Jesus' name, Amen.

The chaffing of change can challenge us to find liberty in the unchanging, faithful God.

Meditation - Opposition Brings Growth

Praying Psalm 5: O Lord, hear me as I pray each morning. I bring my requests to you. Deal with any pride, so I can stand in your presence. I take shelter and protection in you, spread your protection over all who love your name.

Scripture Text - Acts 4:1-4
But many who heard the message believed; so the number of men who believed grew to about five thousand. Acts 4:4

    None of us like to face opposition or difficulties in life. Often, as we get older, the realities of our physical strength and condition can be troublesome and problematic. When we are younger, we feel we are invincible. Peter and John did not likely feel invincible, but they were given boldness to share the good news about Jesus. This boldness resulted in two different responses: they were seized and put into prison and later faced trial (verse 3); secondly, we read, "Many who heard the message believed." This good news/bad news response to God's love still occurs today. Even in dark and difficult times, God plans for us to experience growth, perseverance, fervent faith, and trust in God. Growth requires our willingness to surrender to God. What challenges or difficulties lie before you today? They might be relational challenges, financial limitations, physical restrictions or difficulty. Do you face opposition because of your faith in Jesus? Take heart: opposition brings growth.

Suggested Song:
"Take My Life and Let It Be Consecrated, Lord to Thee"

Pray: Loving God, I know that you long to see growth in my life. Sometimes this can be painful. Thank you for the encouragement from your Word about growth coming through opposition and difficult times. Give me strength, grace, and the willingness to surrender to you in all things. In Jesus' name, Amen.

Cloudburst, Ray

Meditation – Boldly

Praying Psalm 6: Have compassion on me, for I am weak. Save me in your unfailing love. Drive all evil away from me; for you Lord have heard my weeping.

Scripture Text - Acts 4:23-31
After they prayed, the place where they were meeting was shaken. And they were all filled with the Holy Spirit and spoke the word of God boldly. Acts 4:31

This text gives us an amazing example of praying boldly. Often, when we are in trouble, we pray for strength, peace, guidance, and patience. These are all good prayer requests. However, there are times when we need to raise our voice and pray that God gives us holy boldness. Prayer is powerful. Some have even referred to prayer as being subversive. God is sovereign (verse 24). God holds the nations and individual leaders in his hand. Jesus, the anointed one, demonstrated his power and reliance on prayer. The Holy Spirit works in and through our prayers. Does anything need shaking up in your life? Pray. Be sure to pray together with others as well. Verse 24 encourages us as we see the people "raise their voices together in prayer to God." Find a few Christian friends to join you in praying boldly for the needs of the world. The outcome of prayer in Acts 4 is the Holy Spirit providing power to speak the word of God boldly.

Suggested Song: "Lord, Listen to Your Children Praying"

Pray: Loving God, I want to be a person who prays more boldly. Thank you for the examples of these early Christians who faced adversity with an outlook to spread the healing power and convicting message of forgiveness through Jesus Christ. I pray for pastors, leaders, teachers, and myself, that we will all seize opportunities to be bolder in our faith. In Jesus' name, Amen.

Christmas Pageant at Tabor Home

In the interest of full disclosure, I got the idea from another care home in our city. Residents beautifully garbed in Christmas pageant attire – shepherds, magi, Mary, and Joseph, all stationed appropriately in the Bethlehem birth story setting. The narrative from Luke 2 was read, interspersed by poems, songs, and stories. Many residents participated. It was moving – and fun watching "backstage" in Court View Dining Room while everyone was readied for their parts: a husband and wife being Mary and Joseph, Mary in a blue shawl, Joseph looking suitably nervous, a few angels with halos slightly askew. Maureen asked, "How did I get myself into this?" How do any of us get into the picture? God's grace, reliving that holy night.

In the Fullness of Time

It's here! The time is come –
Advent days a portal to the first day,
In the first Light and still night.
Measuring time is helpful for humans.
Grains of sand in hourglass
or digital LED pixels,
Lunar calendars or
galactic Hubble tracked sky space.
In the fullness of time God sent his Son.
Mary had her promise and proof,
she magnified in praise.

Holy Spirit hovers, covers cosmos and womb.
It's time: 200 years since *Stille Nacht* debut at Saint Nicholas parish church,
2,000 years since *gloria in excelsis*.
Different tongues for different times.
Everything beautiful in its own time.
A time for every purpose under heaven.

Daily I tumbled the Advent blocks numbering the days, until tonight reads 01.
It's about time: Church year, Julian Calendar
Ordered time with a heart of wisdom -
It's time.

Meditation – Generosity

Praying Psalm 7: Lord, I pray for justice for those persecuted by enemies, for those wickedly oppressed, in poverty, marginalized by race, culture or religion. Forgive me for being indifferent, ignoring and prejudging from my life of privilege. Arise, O Lord, in anger!

Scripture Text - Acts 4:32-37
Joseph, a Levite from Cyprus, whom the apostles called Barnabas (which means "son of encouragement"), sold a field he owned and brought the money and put it at the apostles' feet. Acts 4:36-37

Most of us know at least one generous person, the kind of person who gives freely and openly to church, community, and individuals in need. Barnabas was such a person. He gave of his resources, of his time and energy to be an encourager to others. There are a few basic principles in generosity that we see in this passage: Barnabas viewed his possessions as a gift from God to be shared and distributed for the blessing of others. He was willing to surrender the use and allocation of his money. He "put it at the apostles' feet." And Barnabas did this all for the good of the larger community. The result was that people's lives were blessed, and the gospel was proclaimed. This early example of community did not persist as an ongoing reality throughout Christian history. It is not included in scripture as a command for how to live in community, but it is a beautiful and powerful example of sharing, caring, and selflessness that builds the body of Christ.

Suggested Song:
"Freely, Freely You Have Received"

Pray: Heavenly Father, I long to be a generous person. Thank you for the example of Barnabas. He was a living model of Proverbs 11: 23: "One person gives freely yet gains even more; another person withholds unduly and comes to poverty." Open my heart, my mind, and my resources to extend your love and help to others. In Jesus' name, Amen.

Ice Storm, Ray

Meditation – Deception

Praying Psalm 8: O Lord our Lord, how majestic is your name in all the earth. I join with children and infants to praise you. Compared with the work of your fingers, the moon, the stars, who am I? Helps us frail humans to be better stewards. Lord, our Lord, WOW!

Scripture Text - Acts 5:1-10
You have not lied just to human beings but to God. Acts 5:4b

Telling the truth is something we need to learn as children and to put into practice in every relationship throughout our life. If we cannot believe that a person is telling us the truth, we continually live with doubt, skepticism, and distrust. The fundamental issue in this tragic episode in the life of the early church is that this husband and wife tried to deceive the community, and foolishly thought that they could deceive God. Apparently, they wanted to appear more generous and altruistic than they were willing to be. They didn't need to give the whole amount. But when they lied by saying that the gift was complete, they were lying not only to the apostles but to God. No one can lie to God. We may not be struck dead as Ananias and Sapphira were, but part of us dies inside our spirit every time we try to deceive. Jesus said, "Let your yes be yes and your no be no." (Matthew 5:37) Lying destroys relationships.

Suggested Song: "Trust and Obey"

Pray: My Lord and my God, may every word I speak be the truth. Jesus, you are the Way, the Truth and the Life. I want to dwell in Truth. In Jesus' name, Amen.

Day and night meditate, contemplate, ruminate, chew over the teachings of God's truth – round the clock, in every season. (Psalm 1)

Meditation - Make Me a Servant

Praying Psalm 9: I will give thanks to you, Lord, with all my heart; I will tell of all your wonderful deeds. I will be glad and rejoice in you; you reign forever; have mercy on me. Let the nations be judged in Your presence.

Scripture Text - Acts 6:1-7
Brothers and sisters, choose seven men from among you who are known to be full of the Spirit and wisdom. We will turn this responsibility over to them. Acts 6:3

I worked with a colleague who was always willing to serve others. We would joke together as we walked down the hall as to who could open the door first for the other to enter. As we did, we hummed the little song, "Make me a servant, humble and meek. Lord, let me lift up those who are weak." In our culture, acts of service, meekness, and surrender are seen as a weakness. Jesus said in his "upside-down" manifesto we call the Sermon on the Mount, "Blessed are the meek for they will inherit the earth." (Matthew 5:5) Yet, when twelve individuals were chosen to serve, a very important community function, they were granted high recognition. They were seen as people "full of the Spirit and wisdom." When we sit down in a restaurant, or when we go into a store, or a service centre to have our car repaired, we are greeted by people who are prepared to serve. The church needs people who are willing to serve. It is a high calling to serve.

Suggested Song: "Make Me a Servant"

Pray: Lord, please forgive me for the times of arrogance and insensitivity that led me to be dismissive of those who are serving me. Grant me a spirit of humility, meekness, and give me eyes to see the needs around me today. In Jesus' name, Amen.

Home for Christmas

My first Christmas as chaplain I came to the Home with the Executive Director and the two of us walked from room to room singing Christmas songs. "Jingle Bells," "White Christmas," *"Feliz Navidad."* I sang some of the Christmas classics – "Joy To The World" and "Silent Night." Christmas 2017 was made even more meaningful and fun for me as I later attended our family celebration, because of the joy I had seen on the faces of my Tabor friends. Many residents had family with them on that Christmas morning, the halls were decorated with festive displays, and the atmosphere was warm and homey. Home for Christmas.

To Merge With Her Molecules

> slipping through the tight molecules
> is that how it happens?
A re-gathering, regrouping, re-membering?
Or a new constellation configuration?
> Jesus walked with the sad travellers
> and talked about himself: from ordering
> chaos to the day he moved into the neighborhood
> and beyond.
Passing, pressing molecules in free float
waving them aside like Jedi or Neo
not a patter or pummel, but warm droplets
bathe, soak, renew, refresh.
> Mary invited this Presence
> to merge with her molecules
> flesh of flesh, light of light
> until she gently wrapped Him in
> strips of cloth – a foreshadow.
Once unwrapped he walks and talks, sits and eats
With you. With me.

Meditation - Let it Shine

Praying Psalm 10: Why, Lord, do you stand so far away from me? Hidden, silent despite the wickedness around? I despise the evil I see in my world; this world doesn't believe in you; they believe if you exist you have closed your eyes. Rise up! Help! Hear!

Scripture Text - Acts 6:15 – 7:3
All who were sitting in the Sanhedrin looked intently at Stephen, and they saw that his face was like the face of an angel. Acts 6:15

Our life changes as we focus on Jesus. Stephens's face shone "like the face of an Angel" (verse 15). At Tabor Home, as I shared daily morning devotionals, I made a point of looking into the eyes and faces of those who were gathered. Admittedly, many had their eyes closed and were apparently sleeping. On one occasion, after the morning devotional, one of the residents said to me, "My eyes may be closed but my heart is open." Appearances can be deceiving, but usually our faces show what we are thinking and feeling. Emotions of joy, celebration, happiness are evident. Sometimes the emotions of anger, frustration, disappointment, show. Stephen's life had been transformed by the love and forgiveness of Jesus, and it showed on his face. As he shared the old story of salvation recorded in Torah, it became a new story, a living testimony. The old story of Israel being redeemed and led by God became a new reality, and it showed in the face of Stephen. As you go through this day let the glory of Jesus be seen in your life, words, and actions.

Suggested Song: "Turn Your Eyes upon Jesus"

Pray: Father God, may your joy and peace be evident in my life today even when frustrations or disappointments come. May your Spirit in my life reflect the freedom I have experienced in Jesus. May it show on my face, in Jesus' name, Amen.

Gyroscope of Grace:
prevenient and providential;
saving and sending;
teaching and transforming
in ceaseless wheeling circles.

Meditation - Damascus Road

☀ **Praying Psalm 11:** I trust in you, Lord. I won't fly from trouble like a bird. You are in your holy temple; you see all, know all, judge all. You hate violence. You love justice.

📖 **Scripture Text** - Acts 9:1-18
As he neared Damascus on his journey, suddenly a light from heaven flashed around him. Acts 9:3

This account of the conversion of the apostle Paul from the persecutor to an Apostle, from Saul to Paul, is told three times in the book of Acts. It is one of the most dramatic and significant examples of what happens when God calls us to follow him. Some of us have had dramatic conversion experiences. Many of us, however, have had more gradual change in our lives as we seek to become more and more obedient to God. We celebrate each person's individual journey. While we often focus on the celebrity, in this case Paul, there are many actors in each of our lives. If it were not for Ananias (verse 17) and his obedient courage to follow God's directions, we may never have heard the story of Paul and his dramatic conversion. Today, be faithful in the small details and be obedient when you sense God calling you to action. You might be another Ananias in someone's life.

🎵 **Suggested Song:**
"Make Me a Blessing"

🙏 **Pray:** Heavenly Father, I want to be obedient to you today in whatever you call me to do. Thank you for both Paul and Ananias. Thank you for the examples of strong leaders, and faithful, obedient servants. Guide me today. May I be a blessing in someone's life, and may you receive the glory, in Jesus' name, Amen.

Blue Flowers, Nixon

Meditation - Prayer Changes Things

⚞☀⚟ **Praying Psalm 12:** Help, Lord, for the godly are few and far between. Everyone is lying to their neighbour. Your words are flawless. Protect the needy.

📖 **Scripture Text** - Acts 12:5-7
So Peter was kept in prison, but the church was earnestly praying to God for him.
Acts 12:5

One of my desires as the chaplain of Tabor Village during my time serving the community was to make Tabor a community of prayer. When people asked me, "What can I do for the kingdom of God now that I am so old?" I would answer in different ways for different individuals, but I always included the challenge to pray. Pray first. Pray without ceasing. Prayers of praise, thanksgiving, and intercession should always rise to heaven. In the text today, we read how the church was earnestly praying to God for Peter in prison. This prayer was answered in a miraculous way. It resulted in freedom, boldness, and a deeper faith. The ministry of prayer in our churches can never be overemphasized. Chains fall off when we as God's people pray. As we would often pray the Lord's Prayer at Tabor, the phrase, "Your will be done, Your Kingdom come on earth as in heaven," was a repeated intercessory prayer. Are there any chains in your life that you need removed? Take it to the Lord and ask other Christian friends to pray for you.

🎵 **Suggested Song:** "What a Friend We Have in Jesus"

🙏 **Pray:** Loving Heavenly Father, your will be done today on earth, in my life, in my church, in my city, as it is in heaven. Thank you for the freedom and release you offer me today. I pray in Jesus' name, Amen.

Liminal Conversations

Henry lived in Tabor Court. He was a quiet man who was friendly but reserved. We would greet one another before service, and he would always say a few words to me at the door as he was leaving. I was quite surprised one day when he looked at my white goatee and my brownish hair and said with a smile, "I'd never trust a man, even if he was my brother, if his hair is one colour and his beard another." After that joke we would have frequent conversations of reflection, encouragement, and thoughtful challenge. I have used the hair-colour joke with others a few times since. (I'm always looking for new material.)

Drawn To the Light

Drawn to the light, drawn to the Light.
Not our own strength, not our own might.
Dimly, in flickers, now bursts in full sight.
Image and Metaphor: dawning from night.
Evening and morning, daylight from dark,
God works while we rest; sets the first spark.
Soon flaming like fire in forest or park
Light Source creates pockets of shadow stark.
Wise ones still seeking heaven's epiphany.
Light show, night show a visual symphony.
Noiseless and still or with cymbals and timpani
God in the shadows still leaves a gift for me.
Yet, drawn to amusements or things that will please us
We work dawn to dusk, still happiness flees us.
Suddenly, shockingly; or with subtle increases
Insight, Divine Light; Joy-filled, time freezes -
Drawn to the light, the light of Jesus.

Meditation - One of the Shepherds

Praying Psalm 13: How long, O Lord? Will you forget me forever? Answer me! I choose to trust in your steadfast love, to rejoice in you, and sing to you – for your salvation and bountiful blessings.

Scripture Text - Amos 1:1-2
The LORD is my shepherd, I lack nothing. Psalm 23:1

The role of shepherds in the Bible is prominent. They are depicted as simple labourers and servants of a greater master. They are people in touch with nature, with the elements of wind, rain, heat, cold. They are also used as a metaphor for great leaders like David. Jesus referred to himself as the Good Shepherd. When Amos the prophet begins his words of judgment and correction for the nation of Israel as one of the Twelve Minor prophets in the Bible, he simply refers to himself as "one of the shepherds of Tekoa." What does it require to be used of God? In the case of this seer, a non-professional prophet, a man of his time and place, it required bold obedience. In our own time and place, we are called to serve God and to serve others around us. Sometimes it requires holy boldness to speak out in our own time and place, but we also are called to be "one of the shepherds." Fortunately, we have a Good Shepherd to follow.

Suggested Song: "The Lord's My Shepherd"

Pray: Heavenly Father, thank you for being my Shepherd, for leading me and guiding me to places of rest and refreshment. You also guide me through dark valleys. I pray for boldness when required, and much love and grace always. In Jesus' name, Amen.

Drawn to the Light, Lyra

Meditation - Seek God – Live

Praying Psalm 14: Fools don't believe in you, Lord. But you see all. Deliver us. We will rejoice and be glad.

Scripture Text - Amos 5:4-6a
"Seek me and live." Amos 5:4b

In my attempt to work through all sixty-six books of the Bible over the course of four years at Tabor Home, there were portions of scripture that were definitely hard to convey to the residents in a way that would be understandable and uplifting. Amos 5 had to be considerably adapted. I only read, *"Seek me and live; do not seek Bethel, do not seek Gilgal, do not journey to Beersheba ... Seek the LORD and live."* I did not spend much time unpacking the associations of ancient places of pagan worship. I did not spend much time dwelling on the theme of national judgment. I focused on the invitation of God to seek Him and find life. This is a message that everyone needs to hear, no matter your age or stage in life. We all tend to be distracted, to seek meaning in life in unhelpful places. This text reminds us to find true life in God alone. Jesus said, "I AM the way, the truth and the life." Seek God today.

Suggested Song: "I Have Decided"

Pray: LORD, in this world there are so many lures and distractions from seeking you and you alone. Forgive me for the many times I have looked for life and meaning apart from you. Thank you for your invitation to seek you, and I do so today in Jesus' name, Amen.

Preachers, prophets, and poets are called to comfort the afflicted and afflict the comfortable. Most days I feel pretty comfortable, even in my affliction.

Meditation - A Hard Reality

Praying Psalm 15: O Lord, who may abide in your tent or dwell on your holy hill? Forgive me, cleanse me, guard my thinking and speaking. I am in awe of your holiness; this directly influences my integrity. Help me stay true to you.

Scripture Text - Amos 5:11-15
Seek good, not evil that you may live. Then the LORD God Almighty will be with you, just as you say he is. Amos 5:14

The call for justice in our day is ringing through our nations. Issues of racial prejudice, Indigenous rights, intolerance, homelessness, and poverty to name just a few. We grieve to see the extent of injustice in our day. In the day of the prophet Amos, we see unfair taxes on the poor (verse 11), inequity of resources, disregard for sinfulness (verse 12), and oppression. The outcry relating to elder care and elder abuse in our society is perhaps unprecedented. Amos instructs his listeners to "*seek good not evil, that you may live.*" Another prophet, Micah, exhorts his generation "*(God) has shown you, O mortal, what is good. And what does the LORD require of you? To act justly and to love mercy and to walk humbly with your God.*" Micah 6:8.

When I shared this text at Tabor Home, I struggled with how I could share such a hard word with people in such a vulnerable time of life. It is a hard word to hear and a difficult reality to face whatever our stage in life.

Suggested Song – "Jesus Calls Us"

Pray: O loving God and Heavenly Father, forgive us for the blatant sins of injustice in our world today. Jesus, you came that we might have life, and have it abundantly. May I be a person of justice, goodness, and compassion, sharing the love of Jesus with everyone I meet. In his name I pray, Amen.

Nice Shirt And Tie

Roy seldom made eye-contact with me. When I tried to engage him in conversation, he either looked away or brushed me off briskly. I respected his desire to not join in a conversation, but I would gently, persistently try in little ways to befriend him. I asked some staff how they connected with him, but those methods didn't seem to work for me. My regular weekday dress clothes were replaced on Sundays with a shirt, tie and suit jacket. As I walked towards Roy that Sunday morning, he said with a stern look, but a twinkle in his eye, "Nice shirt and tie. You should have worn that sooner."

Best Gifts

Journey on with entourage of eastern scholars,
Searchers for meaning of stars and neglected manuscripts;
Longing for adventure:
Advent tour wending toward Epiphany.
Open and prepared to worship,
With questions:
>Where was the One born King?

With resources:
>Frankincense pungent aroma of ascending prayer
>Myrrh resin of resonance for death shroud
>Gold with lustre of wealth, opportunity, Royalty.

Am I prepared to travel – where, how,
Am I bringing all my best gifts
Am I wending my way to I AM?

Meditation - The Straight Truth

⛅ **Praying Psalm 16:** Keep me safe, my God, for in you I take refuge. Help me stay focused on you, my Master, not on the culture around me. You alone are my portion; you have placed my life boundary lines in pleasant places.

📖 **Scripture Text** - Amos 7:7-8
And the LORD asked me, "What do you see, Amos?" "A plumb line," I replied. Then the Lord said, "Look, I am setting a plumb line among my people Israel; I will spare them no longer." Amos 7:8

I have done some home renovations over the years. Working in an old house, one of the most difficult things is trying to work with walls that are no longer true to the plumb line. You have one of two choices: you adapt to the crooked wall, or you tear it down and build new. Several residents of Tabor Home were carpenters and builders. When I asked one of them to give a description of a plumb line, he said something like, "A simple piece of string that does a very important job!" God wants our lives to be straight and true. This requires the work of the Holy Spirit renewing, rebuilding, and reconstructing our lives. Psalm 119: 9: *"How can a young person stay on the path of purity? By living according to your word."* When we apply the straight truth of God's Word to our lives, we build on a solid rock. (Matthew 7:24-27)

🎵 **Suggested Song:** "My Hope is Built"

🙏 **Pray:** Loving God, I want my life to be built on truth and righteousness. Forgive me for allowing deception or lack of faith to lead me down a wrong path. Thank you that your Word is true. I depend on you today for strength, direction, and peace. In Jesus' name, Amen.

Obedience engenders opportunities

Meditation – Bless You

Praying Psalm 17: Show me the wonders of your great love, you who save by your right hand those who take refuge in you. Keep me as the apple of your eye; hide me in the shadow of your wings.

Scripture Text - Matthew 5:1-11
Blessed are the poor in spirit, for theirs is the kingdom of heaven. Matthew 5:3

The Beatitudes are the Prologue to Jesus' Sermon on the Mount (Matthew 5-7). As a Prologue they introduce this Manifesto of Christian faith as laid out and lived out by our Lord. Blessing! It is a word of enrichment, encouragement, flourishing. Some have translated the word as happy. We want to live a life that is blessed by God, so we can live a life that blesses others. To be poor in spirit is to be realistic, humble, and responsive in God's presence. As we admit and accept our personal spiritual poverty before a great and all-powerful God, we are in a proper posture to receive true and everlasting spiritual wealth. Jesus describes it as the Kingdom of heaven! We are all too aware of weakness and "poverty." We see it in infants who need constant care; we see it in elders who need assistance in various ways; we see it in many facets of our human mortality and finitude. But when we admit our poverty and seek Jesus, we are in His kingdom.

Suggested Song: "All To Jesus I Surrender"

Pray: O Lord, I come to you today deeply aware of my need and poverty of spirit. I confess times of spiritual pride and self-righteousness. I receive your blessing today and joyfully enter the Kingdom of Heaven, in Jesus' name, Amen.

Country Church, Ed

Meditation - Happy Mourning

Praying Psalm 18: I love you, Lord, my strength. I call to you for you are worthy of praise, and you have saved me. In my distress I called to you. You heard my voice. These days of darkness, calamity, chaos, you reach out to me and take hold of me. Your way is perfect; humble me, Lord. Provide a broad path for me. Because you live, I praise you, my Rock, Saviour, Fortress, Deliverer, Shield, Strength.

Scripture Text - Matthew 5:12-16
Blessed are those who mourn, for they will be comforted. Matthew 5:4

Jesus said a lot of difficult things. He said, take up your cross and follow me, die to yourself, the last will be first. You're happy when you're sad! Mourning is reflecting on loss. The human emotion of grief is powerful and is a healthy sign of deep love and significant loss. The Beatitudes are a list of "lasts." They are the last things we would think of as "blessed": poverty (verse 3), mourning (verse 4), hunger and thirst (verse 6), but in Jesus' Kingdom we recognize he is turning our everyday expectations upside down. We might say, "right-side-up living in an upside-down world." Perhaps Jesus is also speaking about mourning our sins. In the Old Testament, times of repentance, confession, and grief for sins committed are often expressed by sackcloth and ashes. We need to mourn. We need to mourn the loss of loved ones, and the loss of relationship that our sin causes. The blessing in this Beatitude is that we find comfort in our loving God.

Suggested Song: "Does Jesus Care?"

Pray: Heavenly Father, comfort us as we mourn. Give us strength for each day of our journey. We pray for hope and courage in the day ahead, in Jesus' name, Amen.

Thank You For Being You

Joe was always ready to help and loved to tidy up little messes and assist in any way he could. When I first got to know Joe, he was still quite mobile and able to help with these small jobs. As staff we affirmed him and thanked him for his work. As he aged and mobility became limited, he continued to encourage in any way he could, increasingly with words of affirmation to us as staff. Sometimes we wonder if the things we do in life make a difference. Like Joe, many of us try to just do the little things that may help to make life better for others. One day as we were visiting, he looked at me and said, "Thank you for being you."

Admire a Newborn King

Myrrh provides resin to embalm
Mask the death stench
With aroma of pungent perfume
Admire a newborn King
With this gift of death.
Blur of life
Burial rites; burial rights.

Myrrh provides reason for travel
Common currency of caravan trader
Aroma sent to appease and please
The dimmed and dying sense.

Myrrh provides risen body
With cologne for the Emmaus walk
Scent to be recognized
Sent to break bread with companions.

Meditation – Inheritance

Praying Psalm 19: The heavens speak of your glory – nonstop, around the clock – and everybody hears it! Thank you for today's sunrise and sunset, my Bridegroom. Your law is perfect, I am refreshed. Your statutes, precepts, commands give me joy; more than money, pleasure, power, or recognition; like honey from the honeycomb. May the words of my mouth and the meditations of my heart be acceptable in your sight.

Scripture Text - Matthew 5:21-26
Blessed are the meek, for they will inherit the earth. Matthew 5:5

Our fallen world places inordinate attention on power. Power can become an idol. This is not to say that assuming a role of leadership which is attended by a degree of power and influence is a sin. But we do know that in history, and in the present, there are people who lust after power. Meekness is the opposite of ruthless power. Meekness is humility in action. Jesus humbled himself and became a servant (Mark 10: 45). We are blessed as we humbly serve others. Jesus describes this as a precious inheritance. An inheritance is a gift that we don't deserve or earn. As we follow Jesus' example of meekness, the very thing that people who are pursuing power desire most becomes our inheritance, a gift. Jesus said, *"Learn from me, for I am gentle and humble in heart."* (Matthew 11:29) The posture of someone seeking power is often a clenched fist; the posture required to receive a gift is an open hand and a humble heart.

Suggested Song: "Precious Lord, Take My Hand"

Prayer Heavenly Father, help me today to rely on your strength, your power, and not my own. I know that your strength is made perfect in my weakness. May I follow Jesus' example today as I seek to be blessed in his humility, in his name I pray, Amen.

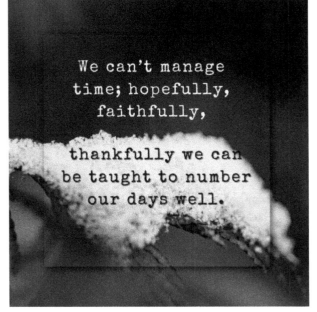

We can't manage time; hopefully, faithfully, thankfully we can be taught to number our days well.

Meditation − Hunger

Praying Psalm 20: Please answer me, Lord. Protect, provide, prosper, for your victory.

Scripture Text - Matthew 5:17-20
Blessed are those who hunger and thirst for righteousness, for they will be filled.
Matthew 5:6

Many older adults have experienced trauma and painful difficulties in their lives. Some of the residents at Tabor Home had known the experience of being refugees. We know that today there are people in Canada who live with painful memories of abuse, injustice, and oppression. Jesus says the desire for righteousness should be as keen and persistent as physical hunger and parching thirst. As followers of Jesus, we believe we are to be the hands and feet of Jesus to those around us. As we go through this day, may we seek to be people of righteousness. This can be as simple and challenging as speaking the truth, living with integrity, being kind, showing care for the lost and hurting in our lives. The promise of this blessing is fulfilment. The lack of contentment in life is a driving force for consumerism. As we seek righteousness, we will be filled and find contentment in Christ Jesus.

Suggested Song: "His Eye is On the Sparrow"

Pray: O God, today I seek contentment in you alone. Give me eyes to see the needs around me, the courage and compassion to help and care for others. As I seek your righteousness and long for it, I thank you in advance for the results. In Jesus' name I pray, Amen.

Intersection, Hudson

Meditation - Mercy Rule

Praying Psalm 21: O Lord, may our leaders rejoice in your strength. Grant victories in the domain of justice, racial equality, and grant liberating wholesome prosperity, and blessings. Overpower the evils of prejudice, greed, idolatry, and consumerism.

Scripture Text - Matthew 5:27-31
Blessed are the merciful, for they will be shown mercy. Matthew 5:7

As I served as chaplain in long term care, I would daily see acts of mercy. Care aides, housekeepers, food services, maintenance, nurses, doctors, and many others showed deep care, compassion, and mercy to our beloved members of the Tabor community. This was evidenced in the ways people spoke and acted toward others.

There are blessings in giving and receiving mercy. When I was a young boy, I loved to wrestle with my older brothers. As they were much stronger than I, there were times when I cried out, "Mercy!" They would stop immediately (or else my parents intervened.)

In amateur sports, when one team is totally dominating the other, sometimes the game will be forfeited. We call this "the mercy rule."

When we receive mercy, we know that a gift of love has been extended. Jesus says we are blessed when we show mercy, and we will receive mercy as a blessed gift in return.

Suggested Song: "Showers of Blessing"

Pray: God of mercy, I know that in my life I need your grace, forgiveness, and mercy. I thank you Lord, that even as I offer this prayer I do so with the request, "Lord, in your mercy, hear my prayer." In Jesus' name, Amen.

As a Little Child

It still warms my heart, when I sing or play "Jesus Loves Me," to hear the voices of those in the room join me – simple words to a song that many of us learned as children, words that remind us deep in our spirits of God's love through Jesus, of the reliability of God in the Bible, of the spiritual depth in coming to the Creator as a little child, weak, and relying on divine strength. After singing it, I would sometimes share the story of the great theologian Karl Barth, who when asked of all the biblical and theological study he had done, what was the one central truth that most gripped his soul. His answer: "Jesus loves me, this I know, for the Bible tells me so."

Yarrow Cemetery

two muddy, sodden, rain-filled tracks led in
to cemetery grounds green slick with rain
fresh mounded mud-soil marked the new-dug plain
revealed her earth-bound resting place within.

slip-slide, select the surest path. Begin
a new and ancient rite, an old refrain.
Commit, inter, infer she's only lain
in Yarrow, narrow plot of earth. A *fin* -

and yet, not the end – we know.
Spirit, essence, inner core
endures disinterred to show
Soul-sail beyond this wet shore.

(Reflecting on a rainy-day burial in Yarrow cemetery)

Meditation – Refined

Praying Psalm 22: My God, I thank you, that I personally have never felt forsaken by you – but the psalmist did. Many people today do. Save, hear, answer, give rest. We acknowledge our sinful, sad state. Rescue me from the mouth of the lions!

Scripture Text - Matthew 5:33-42
Blessed are the pure in heart, for they will see God. Matthew 5:8

The process of refining precious metals like gold and silver requires heat and time. There is a story of a young boy visiting a silversmith. As the boy watched the craftsman refining silver, he asked him, "How do you know when the silver is pure?" The silversmith answered, "When I see my reflection in the silver, I know it is pure." When Jesus sees his reflection in our lives, purity, willingness to serve, a desire to humbly surrender, we are being refined in order to see God.

If you are feeling the heat today, it is likely that you are being refined. Maybe temptations to cut corners at work, to be dishonest, to be unkind. Or maybe you struggle with what you watch, read, and hear. As we trust in Jesus for strength, we can be assured that we are being refined. It may be painful. It takes time. It's a long process. But the blessing of seeing God is worth it.

Suggested Song: "Refiner's Fire"

Pray: Heavenly Father, I want to see your face. I long to know you more intimately and to follow you more faithfully. Today as I experience testing, temptations, and trials, may I be faithful to follow you in all I say and do. I pray in Jesus' name, Amen.

Effectiveness and efficiency is ephemeral, faithfulness is eternal.

Meditation – Peacemakers

☀ **Praying Psalm 23:** Lord, you are my shepherd. I lack nothing. Thanks for the security, nourishment, refreshment that you alone can provide. Lead me, Lord, guide me, comfort me. Even when I walk through dark valleys, give me courage and protection. Thank you for your acceptance of me, for blessing, anointing, and the promise of being forever with you in your house.

📖 **Scripture Text** - Matthew 5:43-48
Blessed are the peacemakers, for they will be called children of God. Matthew 5:9

When I shared the Beatitude about being peacemakers, one of the spouses of a resident in the living room came up to speak to me following our morning prayers at Tabor Home. He had been a peacekeeper in Egypt with the Canadian Army during the Suez Canal conflict. He shared some of his memories about being a peacemaker. Difficult memories. We are called by Jesus to be peacemakers in our world. We are to confront aggression and domination with the spirit of childlike confidence in an all-powerful God. Recently, the words to the Henry Wadsworth Longfellow poem, "I heard the Bells on Christmas Day," came to mind. "There is no peace on earth I said, for hate is strong and mocks the song of peace on earth..." Peacekeeping in our world of power politics and aggression seems highly unrealistic and at times even futile. As children of God, we embrace the theme of peace in the face of adversity. Jesus left his disciples with this blessing, *"Peace I leave with you; my peace I give you. I do not give to you as the world gives. Do not let your hearts be troubled and do not be afraid."* John 14:27

🎵 **Suggested Song:** "It Is Well"

🕯 **Pray:** Loving God, in this world of warfare and conflict it sometimes seems an unrealistic aspiration to be a peacemaker. Thank you that through the sacrifice of Jesus, our Prince of Peace, I can know today that I am your child. Lord, make me an instrument of your peace today. In Jesus' name I pray, Amen.

Have Mercy, Ray

Meditation – The Persecuted

Praying Psalm 24: Lord, everything is yours: the earth, the world and all who live in it; you laid the foundations and water flowed. Purify my heart, refine me, so I can ascend your mountain and stand in your holy presence. You are the King of Glory! Enter.

Scripture Text - Matthew 5:10-12
Rejoice and be glad, because great is your reward in heaven, for in the same way they persecuted the prophets who were before you. Matthew 5:12

No one likes to be mistreated. We live in a day when great efforts are being made to address and correct the injustices inflicted on people in the past. This is a good thing, and we pray it will open a good way forward. Today's Beatitude seems counter to everything we think about fair treatment. No one chooses to be persecuted – do they? Well, Christians over the centuries, and around the world today have been persecuted for their confession of faith in Jesus. We pray regularly for brothers and sisters living in places where the Christian faith is illegal and where being found with a Bible or in a worship setting results in severe penalty. So – how can Jesus say, "Be glad?" "Rejoice?" Our text gives one reason: it is the way God's special, chosen agents, the prophets, were treated before us. We are in very good company when we "are persecuted because of righteousness" (verse 10). The other reason is because Jesus was insulted, falsely accused, had all kinds of evil spoken about him falsely – for our salvation.

Suggested Song: "O How He Loves You and Me"

Pray: Today I pray for all who are being persecuted for their witness as a follower of Jesus. May they receive deep and everlasting blessing as they sacrifice for the sake of the gospel. Make me bold to share the love of Jesus with the lost for the glory of God and the extension of your kingdom, Amen.

Let's Go – Now!

The staff had been given prior information about Cam who came with a history of violence and potential anger issues, so I was careful as I met him for the first time. He seemed to be asking me to take him for a walk to the living room. I misunderstood his invitation to come on, "Let's go now," as an invitation for a walk. I realized later he was taunting me for a fight! Later, my music on the guitar could soothe his troubled spirit. By the end of our relationship, I sat by his bedside reading scripture, praying, gently humming, as he peacefully approached his death. A privilege to walk with you Cam.

Water Danced

The heaven-descended dove that day
Brought Three-in-One into play
As water danced around the Sun
A voice declared,
 "My beloved One."

The Baptizer shaking his head in dismay
Would later testify and say,
"I saw the Holy Spirit descend
And rest on the One God did send;
I saw with my own eyes at Jordan that day."

A sign of a new time
The manifest heir
"The dove descending breaks the air" *
Epiphany two for eyes who see
Living Water from Galilee.

*Little Gidding IV, T.S. Eliot

Meditation - What Does God Look Like?

Praying Psalm 25: In you, Lord my God, I put my trust. Show me your ways, Lord, teach me your paths. Remember, Lord, your great mercy and love, for they are from of old. Guard my life and rescue me, do not remember my sins, for I take refuge in you.

Scripture Text - Colossians 1:15-20
The Son is the image of the invisible God, the firstborn over all creation.
Colossians 1:15

Sometimes when we meet a person and know their parents, we might say something like, "You look exactly like your dad." Family resemblance is what we see in our text when we read the Son is the image of the invisible God. This text is likely an early hymn used in worship in the church. It is a grand, magnificent expression of the glory of God (verse 19) and of the wonderful, healing truth of reconciliation (verse 20).

We are taught to pray in the Lord's Prayer: "Our Father." Do we have the likeness of the Father growing in us? We are called to fix our eyes on Jesus, the author and perfecter of our faith. Is the church, the body of Christ, looking more and more like the Author?

This majestic text about the supremacy of the Son of God assures us of the power and presence of Christ. May his beauty be seen in us today.

Suggested Song: "May the Beauty of Jesus Be Seen in Me"

Pray: Lord Jesus, it is my deepest desire to be more and more like you, to see you more clearly, love you more dearly, follow you more nearly day by day. I read of the power, beauty, and glory of Christ, and I ask for your presence and the power of the Holy Spirit to be evident in my life. In Jesus' name, Amen.

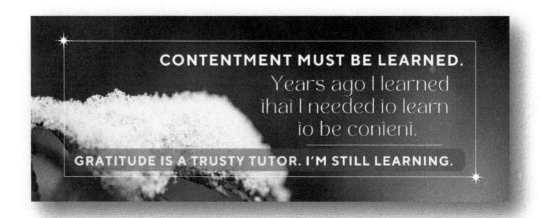
CONTENTMENT MUST BE LEARNED. Years ago I learned that I needed to learn to be content.
GRATITUDE IS A TRUSTY TUTOR. I'M STILL LEARNING.

Meditation - A New Wardrobe

Praying Psalm 26: Lord, I trust in you without wavering; guard my integrity. Prove me, O Lord, and try me; test my heart and mind. O Lord, I love your church, I love to stand in the congregation blessing Your name.

Scripture Text - Colossians 3:12; 15-17; 23,24
Therefore, as God's chosen people, holy and dearly loved, clothe yourselves with compassion, kindness, humility, gentleness and patience. Colossians 3:12

The fashion industry is a multibillion-dollar enterprise. While we should never judge a person by their outward appearance, how a person dresses says something about them. We can identify a police officer and a nurse or firefighter by their clothing. They are wearing their uniform.

Paul is telling us in this passage that we should have a wardrobe that reflects the love, grace, compassion, and humility of Jesus. This should be our uniform. We should be known by these godly traits. The image of clothing ourselves is not to show off how beautiful or fashionable we are, but to display the glory of Christ.

Another text lists similar attributes, describing them as fruit of the Spirit (Galatians 5:22, 23). These new perspectives on life, compassion and humility, replace selfishness and pride. Our motivation for demonstrating kindness, humility, and patience is the love of God. We are God's chosen people, holy and dearly loved (verse 12). People around us will see our "new wardrobe" in our everyday interactions. And when they find out who our Fashion Designer is, they will be encouraged to give thanks and glory to God the Father (verse 17).

Suggested Song: "The Love of God"

Pray: Heavenly Father, I thank you for clothing me with your love, compassion, kindness, and gentleness. As I follow you, Lord, today, I pray for this convicting evidence of your presence in my life. Be glorified in my life today. In Jesus' name, Amen.

Meditation - Dancing and Celebrating

☀ **Praying Psalm 27:** You are my Light and my Salvation. You are my Stronghold – of whom shall I be afraid? Though I have struggles and opposition, yet I will be confident. I only ask to grow closer to you, to see your beauty, to ask you for more of your insight and presence. I wait for you, I take courage in you, I wait for you.

📖 **Scripture Text** - 1 Chronicles 15:25-29
As the ark of the covenant of the LORD was entering the City of David, Michal daughter of Saul watched from a window. And when she saw King David dancing and celebrating, she despised him in her heart. 1 Chronicles 15:29

Corporate worship for the people of God is like breathing – a necessity. When we gather for praise, prayer with a humble posture of submission before our Creator, Redeemer, Sustainer, it is life-giving. David and the entourage were expressing jubilant, joyful praise. Their sacrifice of praise included seven bulls and seven rams (26), singing and instrumental music (27) and dancing and celebration (29). Not everyone understands or appreciates the worship of God, or the methods used. David's wife, who was the daughter of his old enemy King Saul, apparently had issues of her own and she despised David's exuberant expression of worship. In fact, she despised David in her heart (29).

We all worship. Believers and non-believers, churchgoers and agnostics, royalty, and the common folk. What or whom we worship may vary, however. We may worship material things, or personal power, or individual expression – but we all have something before which we express ultimate worth – worth-ship. Maybe Michal despised more than David's dancing and celebration – maybe she despised his God.

🎵 **Suggested Song:** "When Morning Gilds the Skies"

🙏 **Pray:** Lord, I choose again this day to worship you. Forgive me for the times I have worshipped lesser things; remove any idols from my life. May my worship of you be genuine, meaningful, and moving. May it glorify Your name and fame. In Jesus' name, Amen.

My Eyes May Be Closed, But My Heart Is Open."

   Morning prayers in Willow Dining Room were just wrapping up. I was making my visits to each one who had attended. I shared a greeting and had a brief conversation. When I came to Lois, her eyes were closed, as they had been throughout the whole session. I always felt that if I could help residents have a good rest, that was also part of my ministry. Then she opened her eyes and said very clearly, "My eyes may be closed, but my heart is open." That sentiment would encourage me through many sessions when I wondered if the Word, songs, and stories were making a difference in people's hearts.

Winter Beauty, Amy

With Fresh Fruit

The wood-turned bowl on the coffee table
Loaded with fresh fruit –
An unusual sight for my childish eyes
This common, homey gesture.
Real fruit, for the enjoyment of guests
And my recently widowed uncle.
      Love joy, peace
fruit always growing, always showing
the Spirits work in us - aspirational
inspirational, respirational sometimes
perspirational!

      Patience, kindness, goodness
take time, good soil, sunshine and rain
      to produce.
      Faithfulness, gentleness, self-control
All Jesus' virtues:
      "Not my will,"
           "Take my yoke,"
             desert trial.
May this life-giving, refreshing fruit bowl
      find centre place
      in my Living Room.

Meditation – He is Good

☀ **Praying Psalm 28:** To you, O Lord, I call; for if you are silent, I'm as good as in the pit. Hear my prayers. Overcome evil in our systems, our entrenched ways, our arrogant pride. You, Lord, are our strength. Save us. Bless your people, you are our Shepherd.

📖 **Scripture Text** - 2 Chronicles 5:11-14
The trumpeters and musicians joined in unison to give praise and thanks to the LORD. Accompanied by trumpets, cymbals and other instruments, the singers raised their voices in praise to the LORD and sang: "He is good; his love endures forever." Then the temple of the LORD was filled with the cloud. 2 Chronicles 5:13

Over our lives we experience many challenges and disruptions. The COVID-19 pandemic caused many changes to the way we could offer a worship experience for Tabor Home residents. We offered "Hallway Worship" for a while, gathering five or six people at their doorways to the hall for singing, reading and prayer. It was a different kind of worship experience. It became a modified "sanctuary." It was set aside for a different purpose, sanctified for these times of worship. The order of worship was simple. We had no "fine linen" (12), or cymbals, harps or lyres – just my guitar, or device playing songs. Yet in a unique way, it was a place of glory. Bowed heads, whispered prayers, deepened faith stories were unfolding in that hallway worship. We reminded ourselves in those times: *"He is good; his love endures forever."*

Today, may you find and experience a time and place of God's *shekinah* glory. It may be an actual church sanctuary, a chapel or cathedral, but more likely it will be in a more common, everyday space. Maybe in a hallway.

🎵 **Suggested Song:** "A Quiet Place"

🙏 **Pray:** Father God, I want to meet you today and experience a fresh reality of your presence, your grace, your glory. Even if I face unexpected challenges or disruptions, I choose to find opportunities to worship you, for You are good, and your love endures forever. In Jesus' name, Amen.

39

Meditation - Conditional Prayer

Praying Psalm 29: All dimensions of existence praise you, God. We direct all glory to you. This planet has fearsome power: mighty waters, old-growth forests, burning deserts, wilderness above and below. You sit enthroned over flood, drought, turmoil – Lord, please strengthen us and bless us with peace.

Scripture Text - 2 Chronicles 7:11-22
If my people, who are called by my name, will humble themselves and pray and seek my face and turn from their wicked ways, then I will hear from heaven, and I will forgive their sin and will heal their land. 2 Chronicles 7:14

We often speak about unconditional love. We sometimes speak of unconditional acceptance and approval. However, in most relationships there are often healthy conditions to be observed. For example, in relation to our physical bodies, if we treat them well, including regular exercise, nourishing food, adequate rest, and all the other conditions that go into a healthy body, we are more likely to have a body that serves us well.

What about our relationship with God? Are there any conditions applied? Or is God's favour and approval always unconditional? God wants to be in relationship with us. As with any relationships, healthy conditions apply. 1 John 1:7-8: *"If we claim to be without sin, we deceive ourselves and the truth is not in us." If we confess our sins, he is faithful and just and will forgive us our sins and purify us from all unrighteousness.*

Today's verse on prayer lays out clear conditions: humility, earnestly seeking God's face, a desire to live a pure life, then ... Any conditional or covenantal relationship always includes an "if" and a "then." We long for healing. Let us also long to sincerely, humbly seek God with the assurance that "*then* God will hear from heaven, and I will forgive their sin and will heal the land."

Suggested Song: "Great Is Thy Faithfulness"

Pray: Heavenly Father, I ask you to forgive my sins. Grant me the humble confidence to trust in your grace and forgiveness. Oh Lord, heal our land. In Jesus' name I pray, Amen.

Meditation - Give Thanks

Praying Psalm 30: I will extol you, O Lord, for you have drawn me up. I cried to you for help, and you have healed me. Weeping may linger for the night, but joy comes with the morning. You turn mourning to dancing. In you alone I have taken refuge – let me never be ashamed. In your righteousness deliver me. Incline your ear to me. Be to me a rock of habitation to which I may always come. You have provided salvation; you are my rock and fortress.

Scripture Text - 1 Corinthians 1:4-9
I always thank my God for you because of his grace given you in Christ Jesus.
1 Corinthians 1:4

For a person who had experienced so much difficulty in life, the apostle Paul exuded a spirit of gratitude. His prayer for the people he loved and served is inspiring. His prayer was filled with thankfulness, grace, enrichment, and warm advice. And his prayer was regular and ongoing. When we think of the many ways God blesses the church and our world, we have so much to be thankful for. The body of Christ has been gifted with every spiritual gift (verse 7), and the assurance of being loved and kept firm in Christ. God is faithful, we can count on him, and pray with confidence and thankfulness for our world, our church, our leaders, and ourselves.

When I shared this text with the folks at Tabor Home, the theme of the month was life enrichment. While this includes our physical health and wellbeing, our mental wellness, it also includes our spiritual selves. One of the best things we can do for our spiritual self care is to be thankful people.

Suggested Song: "Count Your Blessings"

Pray: Loving God, accept my thanks and appreciation today. I have so much to be thankful for, so many areas of blessing and enrichment that I can only come before you with deep gratitude. Thank you, Lord Jesus, for forgiving me and giving me new life, and it is in your name I pray, Amen.

Love Remembered

Curmudgeonly Bert would hardly make eye-contact. If I said hello, or good morning, he dismissed me gruffly. So, I would usually give him his space, and gradually we began to get along better. I noticed he had a gentle, kind, supportive way with his wife, Edna, as they shared their table at breakfast. After he passed, Edna seemed lost and confused, so we talked about Bert and how he had supported her through their lives together. I came to appreciate a different side of his personality, one which he had difficulty in sharing with others. To encourage Edna after Bert died, I wrote a little poem about how he had loved and supported her. She was overjoyed and placed it on her wall.

From the Heart, Emily

God Only Knows

Did Jesus ever worry?
Did Jesus ever fret?
On tossing sea, in desert match
In Mountain glory – heaven's latch His mansion builder
was not done yet.

Look at the birds, the flowers at ease not harvesting toiling or storing in barns
Not endlessly stressing synthetic yards
Our Father in heaven knows all we need
We fly, we blossom in airfield we are freed.

But what of the garden Gethsemane's sweat
Looking for comforters what did he get?
Sleepers yawning, late night reclining
After Last Supper dining,
His vigil declining.

Keep watch, keep watch the flesh is weak.
But they slept contented
While tree branches creak.
His lessons on worry on having more faith darkened their prayer watch
Like smothering wraith.
Back to his agony three times he goes
It wasn't just worry or lack of repose, it was bloody distress,
Anguish and grief
For what's in the cup
– God only knows!

Matthew 6:26–36; 26:36–42; 26:26–30

Meditation - Love Is

Praying Psalm 31: In you alone I have taken refuge, let me never be ashamed. In your righteousness deliver me, incline your ear to me. Be to me a Rock of Habitation to which I may always come, you have provided salvation, you are my Rock and Fortress.

Scripture Text - 1 Corinthians 13
And now these three remain: faith, hope and love. But the greatest of these is love.
1 Corinthians 13:13

Our world usually sees the word "love" and thinks romance, sentimentality, maybe Valentine's Day. Songs about love fill the airwaves. Movies and novels are filled with love stories. In families we strive to show true love to our children, siblings, and parents.

Today's text is the classic "love chapter" in the Bible. We are reminded that love is action, choice, and character. Love is putting the other person first, considering their needs, their emotional and physical wholeness and well-being (Shalom). And yet, we all have areas of spiritual short-sightedness. We are reminded that now in our daily lives we only see a portion of the greater reality of God's love. Paul expresses it as a mirror (verse 12), which can be a very narcissistic, selfish tool. Faith gives us a firm foundation, hope orients us toward a brighter future, and love sees us through our earthly lives and into an eternal future in God's presence. God is love.

Suggested Song: "The Love of God"

Pray: Thank you, God, for people in my life who love me. Thank you for the gift of love in relationships. Give me eyes to see clearly, desire to love you more dearly, and courage to follow you more nearly day by day, in Jesus' name, Amen.

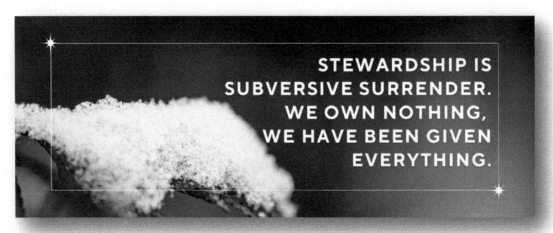

STEWARDSHIP IS SUBVERSIVE SURRENDER. WE OWN NOTHING, WE HAVE BEEN GIVEN EVERYTHING.

Meditation - Jars of Clay

Praying Psalm 32: In you I find true joy, for you have forgiven transgressions. I acknowledge my sin to you; keeping silent was killing me. In times of distress save me from the rush of mighty waters. I rejoice in your steadfast love.

Scripture Text - 2 Corinthians 4:7-9
But we have this treasure in jars of clay to show that this all-surpassing power is from God and not from us. 2 Corinthians 4:7

When I was in high school, I used to make pottery. We had a very gifted and generous art teacher who had developed a good ceramics studio with several wheels for throwing pottery as well as kilns and all the accessories. Our teacher would let us do everything from making the pottery, preparing it for the kiln, glazing it when ready, but would take care of the tasks that were particularly difficult, and that could result in shards of clay.

In Bible times, pottery was used for everyday household tasks. To carry water, to prepare and store foods, and for personal hygiene uses. These jars of clay were fragile and common. Paul uses this metaphor of jars of clay, showing God's surpassing power, and displaying our everyday weaknesses. The text also continues with assuring words that we are not abandoned, struck down or destroyed (verse 9). Our mortal journey begins in infancy where we are totally reliant on adults around us. Throughout our lives we need people supporting and helping us. As we age, we may need different kinds of help. But God is our Refuge and Strength through all the days and years of our lives.

Suggested Song: "What A Friend We Have In Jesus"

Pray: Thank you, God, that your power and strength is made perfect through my weakness. Thank you that this fragile jar of clay, my life and gifts, can be used in your Kingdom. Use me today, I pray, to bless and love others, proclaiming Jesus in word and deed. In Jesus' name, Amen.

Vertical
BY AMY BERGEN

Meditation - Amazing Grace

☀ **Praying Psalm 33:** I rejoice in you, Lord. I praise you with a new song. Your Word creates everything. Your counsel stands forever, your thoughts to all generations.

📖 **Scripture Text** - 2 Corinthians 12:7b-10
But (God) said to me, "My grace is sufficient for you, for my power is made perfect in weakness." Therefore I will boast all the more gladly about my weaknesses, so that Christ's power may rest on me. 2 Corinthians 12:9

The hymn "Amazing Grace" is one song that most people in our Western culture are still familiar with. Many people don't know the old hymns, but "Amazing Grace" can connect with people in different times and phases of their lives. The composer John Newton was a sea captain. He worked for many years in the corrupt, despicable slave trade. After turning his life over to God, his ways changed radically, and he eventually became a pastor. The opening line of this familiar hymn, "Amazing Grace, how sweet the sound that saved a wretch like me," takes on new and richer meaning when you think it was composed by a sailor. Newton was thinking of a safe, sheltered harbour, a body of water which we sometimes refer to as a "sound". We all need to find safe shelter from the storms of life. God's grace is sufficient no matter what challenges we face. Paul reminds us that, when we are weak, we are strong in Christ (verse 10).

🎵 **Suggested Song:** "Amazing Grace"

🙏 **Pray:** Dear God of grace and shelter, I need your protection today. Keep me from the harm of evil, and the weakness of fear and anxiety. Thank you that your grace is more than sufficient to save even me. I pray with thanksgiving for your grace, in Jesus' name, Amen.

The Accordion

As chaplain I had the privilege of meeting many interesting people from all over the world. One was Charles, who had taught himself to play the accordion. He told me how he used to play in a band on Saturday nights at the community centre in his small town near Nelson, BC. Charles would play one of his dance tunes for me and we would chat about his life and love for music. I asked if he knew any hymns, but he quietly replied, "I'm not much of a church man." One day I brought my guitar to his room to play along, and I played "Amazing Grace." Charlie chorded along.

Three Haiku From the Book of Daniel

stumped by his tree dream
proud King learns new math counting
seven on all fours
(Daniel chapter 4)

before the hand writes
before the message is heard
know what time it is
(Daniel chapter 5)

some things can't be changed
the law of Medes and Persians
prayer in upper room
(Daniel chapter 6)

Meditation - Feel the Heat

☀ **Praying Psalm 34:** I will always bless you, Lord; always I boast in you alone. I seek you and you answer me. I listen. Lord, teach me reverence. You keep your eye on the righteous, you are near the broken-hearted and those crushed in spirit. Redeem my life; I seek to serve you.

📖 **Scripture Text** - Daniel 3:24-28
Then Nebuchadnezzar said, "Praise be to the God of Shadrach, Meshach and Abednego, who has sent his angel and rescued his servants! They trusted in him and defied the king's command and were willing to give up their lives rather than serve or worship any god except their own God." Daniel 3:28

Sometimes we feel the heat for decisions we make. If the decisions are to help others or improve quality of life, or to be obedient to God's Word, we need to be willing to accept whatever persecution may come.

A favourite Bible story is about three brave young men who stood up for their beliefs in God. The result was a conversion experience for a powerful, hateful king.

This story has at least three miracles. The first is the appearance of a fourth man walking in the fiery furnace (verse 25). The second miracle is that Shadrach, Meshach and Abednego came out of the fire without a singe or burn (verse 27). The third miracle, surely, is the dramatic change in Nebuchadnezzar. Anytime a person repents and turns around and decides to worship God, we must say that a miracle has occurred.

Maybe a fourth miracle in this story is that people were willing to feel the heat. Counting the cost, these would be martyrs who still obeyed God. Let us be people who have boldness and let us remember people today who are suffering because they are followers of Jesus.

🎵 **Suggested Song:** "Trust and Obey"

🙏 **Pray:** Loving God, today I pray for men and women around the world who are being persecuted because of their faith in Jesus. May they be bold in their witness. May they also be supported by their community of faith and by us who live in countries of relative freedom to worship God. In Jesus' name I pray, Amen.

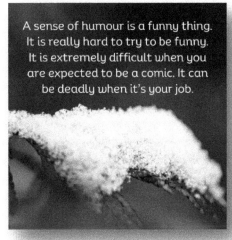
A sense of humour is a funny thing. It is really hard to try to be funny. It is extremely difficult when you are expected to be a comic. It can be deadly when it's your job.

Meditation – *Shema*

Praying Psalm 35: Stand up for me against all enemies, O Lord. Contend with them. You deal with them. I trust in you. You are my shield, armor, spear, and javelin. You are my salvation. How long, O Lord? Do not be absent. You see all. Awake and rise. Be exalted; you delight in the well-being of your servant.

Scripture Text - Deuteronomy 6:1-9
Hear, O Israel: The LORD our God, the LORD is one. Love the LORD your God with all your heart and with all your soul and with all your strength. Deuteronomy 6:4-5

The Hebrew word *Shema* is from our verses from Deuteronomy, "Hear, O Israel." These verses have been used as a teaching tool for children and for followers of Yahweh and are still resonant with us today. Sometimes we need someone to call us to attention.

Our lives become so easily distracted with many things. This call helps us refocus. It is in the context of Moses' teaching about the decrees and the laws of the Lord (verse 1). Obedience requires discipline. When we do something regularly, it becomes a discipline in our lives.

This call to worship the One God became a family tradition (verse 7). The practice of having Bible verses or encouraging texts on plaques on our walls in our homes comes from this teaching.

Today, families compete with media of all kinds demanding our attention. We need to encourage parents as they try to instill Godly principles and practices in their children's lives. And as we grow older, we also need to be daily called to attention to listen, to hear God's word for us.

Suggested Song: "Wonderful Words"

Pray: Thank you, loving Heavenly Father, that today I have taken time to listen to your voice. I read your word, I am encouraged to worship with all my heart, soul, and strength the one and true God. Help me to encourage others in my life to hear Your voice. I pray in Jesus' name, Amen.

Meditation - Pisgah's Peak

☀ **Praying Psalm 36:** O God, you observe the wrongdoers. Your righteousness is like the highest mountains, your justice like the great deep. You, Lord, preserve both people and animals; with you is the fountain of life. In your light we see light.

📖 **Scripture Text** - Deuteronomy 34:1-4
Then Moses climbed Mount Nebo from the plains of Moab to the top of Pisgah, across from Jericho. There the LORD showed him the whole land. - Deuteronomy 34:1

Moses was old. Yet he still had the strength to climb from plain to peak. When we're on an elevated place, whether a mountaintop or a tall building, the perspective and view of everything around us changes. Our physical eyesight does not change, but everything looks different. Moses needed to be reminded and encouraged about the promises of God to the people. Pisgah peak represents those times in our lives when we get a fresh perspective on life, ministry, and opportunities that face us. When we are young, we need the mountaintop experiences to inspire and shape us. As we age, we need to gain renewed perspectives on God's love, grace, and his grand story of salvation through Jesus Christ.

Maybe you are feeling discouraged about what you perceive to be an unfulfilled promise in your life. Trust in God, knowing that He keeps His promises in His timing, and keep climbing!

🎵 **Suggested Song:** "Higher Ground"

🔥 **Pray:** God, I thank you for this reminder of your promises made to your people. May I keep climbing to gain new and fresh vistas of your plans for my life and in the world, in history and in my everyday walk. In Jesus' name, Amen.

Gifted People

I try to avoid asking a person of any age, "What do you do?" I'm more interested in finding out about what is significant in the person's life – what give them joy?
Sometimes when you ask older adults what they did for work, they can't remember, which can be frustrating, even distressing. I enjoy talking with people about their gifts - gardening, cooking, music, art, stories, and relationships. The world is filled with gifted people.

Praying Psalm 37: Do not fret because of those who are evil or be envious of those who do wrong. Trust in the Lord and do good. Commit your way to the Lord. Take delight in the Lord and he will give you the desires of your heart. Be still before the Lord and wait patiently for him. The meek will inherit the earth. Hope in the Lord and keep his way.

Fiddler's Green, quilt created in honor of Mabel Harris

One In Every Crowd
BY RAY HARRIS

SPRING
March – May

If I Could Eavesdrop

If only I could eavesdrop on those
blazing conversations, words of light
illuminating dark pre-Easter crevices.
Word linking word with Word
a formula for new life: for fearful,
angry disciples – and for me.

"Beginning with Moses and the Prophets"
Jesus gave those forty-day seminars
whenever he arrived –
through solid walls and locked doors
or in open-air seaside barbecue
asking leading questions
leading askers to new synapses
connecting Shepherd to sheep
and a Corn King story
takes on resurrection glory.
Still scarred for life – my life,
and by hook or by crook (by rod and staff)
leading, guarding,
guiding, saving
and gently laying his foolish sheep
on his shoulders
rejoicing on the homeward trail.
All we, like sheep have gone astray – Good Shepherd lead.

Meditation - God's Handiwork

Praying Psalm 38: Lord, do not rebuke me in your anger or discipline me in your wrath. My guilt has overwhelmed me. I am bowed down and brought very low. I groan in anguish of heart. All my longings lie open before you, my sighing is not hidden from you.

Scripture Text - Ephesians 2:4-10
For we are God's handiwork, created in Christ Jesus to do good works, which God prepared in advance for us to do. Ephesians 2:10

Everything begins with God. "In the beginning, God…" we read in Genesis 1. God's great love for us and his rich mercy have made us alive with Christ, Paul says in our text. God is Creator and re-Creator. Everything is from the Creator's grace, expressed to us through creation, scripture, and most amazingly, through Jesus Christ. Through this grace our Creator invites us to be sub-creators.

We are God's "handiwork," we are expressions of creativity. As we are created in God's image, let everything we do and say be done with the beauty, creativity, imagination, and joy we see in God our Heavenly Father.

We may point to our favourite artists, authors, architects, and musicians and say, "They are truly creative." And yet, today's text is telling us that we are created in Christ Jesus to do good works.

The way we speak and the way we live are all to display God's creativity.

Be creative. Be imaginative.

Suggested Song: "Take My Life and Let It Be Consecrated"

Pray: Thank you, dear Lord, that you are the Divine Creator. As your handiwork today, help me to consecrate every word, deed, thought, and motive to you, my God. May your imagination and endless artistry be seen in me – to the encouragement of others, and to Your glory. In Jesus' name I pray, Amen.

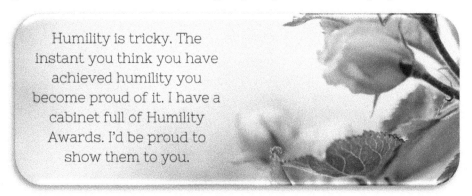

Humility is tricky. The instant you think you have achieved humility you become proud of it. I have a cabinet full of Humility Awards. I'd be proud to show them to you.

Meditation - Servants of God

Praying Psalm 39: Dear God, keep me in your way, put a muzzle on my mouth, keep my tongue from sin. Show me, Lord, my life's end, and the number of my days and how fleeting my life is. Surely everyone goes around like a mere phantom. In vain they rush about, heaping up wealth without knowing whose it will be. But now, Lord, what do I look for? My hope is in you.

Scripture Text - Ephesians 3:7-13
His intent was that now, through the church, the manifold wisdom of God should be made known to the rulers and authorities in the heavenly realms. Ephesians 3:10

God intends the church to make known God's wisdom. This wisdom is the good news of Jesus demonstrated in the gospel. Paul, the servant of the Lord, was given gifts by God's grace to proclaim the good news about forgiveness of sins and new life in Christ. He served God by planting churches and travelling extensively to share the gospel and encourage believers.

I am so thankful for the servants in our churches today. For leaders, teachers, preachers, ushers, children's workers, youth leaders, and the list goes on. I am thankful for today's church-planters all around the world.

The life-changing service of sharing the good news is often difficult. Paul says in this text that it is only through the working of God's power in him that he was able to preach about the boundless riches of Christ (verse 8). Paul reminded the church not to be discouraged because of his suffering (verse 13).

As you serve today, have courage and don't be disappointed with challenges and setbacks. We are all servants of the King.

Suggested Song: "Ye Servants of God"

Pray: Heavenly Father, thank you for those who are leaders in my church. Give them strength, wisdom, determination, and faith as they continue to serve in your Kingdom. Bless me today as I serve all who you bring into my life, in Jesus' name I pray, Amen.

Meditation - Unity

Praying Psalm 40: I wait patiently for you, Lord; you turn to me and hear my cry. You lift me out of the slimy pit and set my feet on rock. You put a new song in my mouth, a hymn of praise to our God. Many, Lord God, are the wonders you have done, none compare with you. Here I am, I have come. I desire to do your will. I proclaim your saving acts; I speak of your faithfulness.

Scripture Text - Ephesians 4:1-7
Make every effort to keep the unity of the Spirit through the bond of peace.
Ephesians 4:3

It takes effort to live in unity. Peacemaking is difficult work. A beautiful prayer is attributed to Saint Francis, "Lord, make me an instrument of Your peace. Where there is injury let me bring pardon..."

There are many reasons why living together in harmony can be difficult. A list of required attributes includes humility, gentleness, patience (verse 2). These are virtues that we desire to cultivate, but we recognize they are fruit of the Holy Spirit in our lives. As we remain in Christ, God brings this fruit into our relationships and communities.

We often speak about unity in diversity. Being united in Christ certainly does not mean we are all carbon copies of one another. Each one of us, in God's grace, has been given unique talents, personalities, and spiritual gifts. As we are called to live in community, in our families, in our homes, in our workplaces, and in the church, we each exercise our God-given uniqueness – so that we may be one.

Suggested Song: "We Are One in the Spirit"

Pray: Lord, make me an instrument of your peace. I pray for my city, province, country, and the world. Global peace has never been a human reality throughout history. As a follower of Jesus, may I bring Your peace that passes all human understanding into my world. In Jesus' name, Amen.

I Am Here to Pray

Frequently, conversations at Tabor Home include the question, "Why am I still here?" "What good am I now?" We all need a feeling of worth, purpose, and meaning in life, and as we age, we sometimes lose that – and we need to refocus it. I choose to ask people questions like, "What do you enjoy doing?" "What gives you satisfaction?" "How can you make other people smile, or laugh?" Sometimes this opens the discussion to things like providing encouragement to others, being grateful, being humble and willing to not take ourselves too seriously. Often it turns to prayer. "I can still pray." "Maybe that's why I'm still here!" This is an awakening for any and all of us.

Pillar of Fire, Ray

A Beautiful Thing

an alabaster jar
  translucent, creamy white
  milk-coloured container
of very expensive perfume
  aromatic, fragrant oil
   ointment of the ancients
 pure nard
she broke the jar and poured.
  wasteful, haste-full extravagance
   lavish love laving
prodigal burial preparation
the perfume on his head
  precious ointment
in capite quod descendit *
(like precious ointment on his head)
ironic, Aaronic!
she has done a beautiful thing
  to Me
...in memory of Me
   in memory of her...
broken, poured-out, pungent
costly pure nard
burial preparation,
and High Priest anointing

*Psalm 133:2 in Latin

Meditation - Please Send Someone Else

☀ **Praying Psalm 41:** Dear Creator God, you bless those who have regard for the weak. You deliver them in times of trouble. O Lord, protect and preserve them. Opponents whisper together against me; everyone turns against me. Uphold me in integrity.

📖 **Scripture Text** - Exodus 4:1-13
But Moses said, "Pardon your servant, Lord. Please send someone else." Exodus 4:13

Have you ever argued with God? Have you ever had the clear sense that God wants you to perform some task, but you just don't want to do it? Maybe we are afraid. Maybe the request will take us out of our comfort-zone.

Moses, that great servant of the Lord, makes five objections to God's call. He concludes with a plea, "Please send someone else."

God had even provided three miraculous signs to assure Moses that God would go with him on his assigned task. The shepherd's staff was turned into a snake (verse 3), instantaneous leprosy appeared (verse 6), then disappeared (verse 7). God promised to provide even more dramatic signs if these first three did not suffice. Moses kept making excuses.

I am reluctant like Moses sometimes. I want to be obedient, but often fear of rejection or misunderstanding stops me in my tracks. Even with the promise of God's presence, I'm resistant to step out of my comfort-zone. I am encouraged by this account of Moses' reluctance. And I am inspired by Jesus who prayed, *"Father, not my will but yours be done."* (Luke 22:42)

🎵 **Suggested Song:** "Have Thine Own Way Lord"

⚡ **Pray:** Loving God and Heavenly Father, I know that I am more like Moses than like your Son Jesus when it comes to following your call. May my prayer today be "Your will be done," in Jesus' name, Amen.

Humour can bring levity to a heavy situation.
Joy dislodges the gravity of the boulder in relation to God's timing.

Meditation - The Getaway

Praying Psalm 42: As the deer pants for streams of water, so my soul pants for you, my God. When I am downcast and disturbed, I put my hope in you. I will yet praise you, my Saviour, and my God.

Scripture Text - Exodus 12:31–36
During the night Pharaoh summoned Moses and Aaron and said, "Up! Leave my people, you and the Israelites! Go, worship the LORD as you have requested." Exodus 12:31

The story of the Passover, Israel making a getaway at night from their Egyptian taskmasters, is exciting. God-initiated from start to finish. God-directed the details of taking unleavened bread and the voluntary plunder of the Egyptian people. Pharoah and his officials had been merciless to the Jews, but the people of Egypt seemed kindly disposed towards (or deeply fearful of) the escapees. We know that the story continues through the book of Exodus and is rehearsed and celebrated annually. This midnight escapade is full of drama and fear. The Israelites obeyed Moses' God-given direction to place blood on their door frames so that he would pass over, and so they were rescued.

God is still in the business of releasing people from their places of captivity and enslavement. Maybe present-day captivity for some is an addiction, a persistent sin, or being trapped in a cycle of anger or compulsion. Whatever the situation, God still saves and frees us.

With the stunning words of Pharaoh ringing in Moses' ears, "Go, worship the LORD." They made their way out of bondage and worshipped.

Suggested Song: "Redeemed How I Love to Proclaim It"

Pray: Loving Heavenly Father, thank you for forgiveness of sin and for freedom in Jesus. Through Jesus' blood shed on the cross, I have been bought back, redeemed, set free. Help me today in my getaway from bondage, in Jesus' name, Amen.

Meditation – Design

Praying Psalm 43: Vindicate those who seek you, O God. Send me Your light and faithful care, let them lead me and bring me to your holy mountain.

Scripture Text - Exodus 31:1-11
See, I have chosen Bezalel son of Uri, the son of Hur, of the tribe of Judah, and I have filled him with the Spirit of God, with wisdom, with understanding, with knowledge and with all kinds of skills. Exodus 31:2-3

God calls people for specific ministries and gifts them "with knowledge and all kinds of skills..." (verse 3). Bezalel was an artist and a craftsman. As described in Exodus 31, God had very specific designs for the Tabernacle, God's place of worship on the move. It required someone who was not only an accomplished artisan, but one who was "filled with the Spirit of God."

A story is told of someone visiting the construction of a great medieval cathedral. As the person walked through the worksite, they saw three workers. When asked what they were doing, the first worker replied, "I'm just doing my job as a stone mason, so I can feed my family." A second artisan replied, "I am using my skills to build a straight, solid wall." The third stone artist replied, "I am building an awesome cathedral to the glory of God."

God calls and equips you to use your wisdom, understanding, knowledge and skills – to create beauty to the glory of God.

Suggested Song: "My Hope is Built"

Pray: Loving God of beauty and creativity, thank you for gifting people with amazing skill and artistry. I choose to honour you today with my time, talents, and treasures – to enjoy you and give you glory. In Jesus' name, Amen.

Suffering

Growing old, approaching the end of our lifespan can be hard. To experience decline in physical health and cognitive capacity is to endure suffering. Aging is hard work. The problem of suffering can become acute in our old age. We live in a culture that tries to avoid all suffering. We have succeeded in many astounding ways through education, medical advances, and technology to reduce human suffering, but it is still a present human reality. Only once in my time as Tabor's Spiritual Care Coordinator did we have a resident request for medical assistance in dying (MAID). We met with the resident and their family. Tabor has conscientious objector status, so we began to discuss options. In this case, the issues that were causing most acute suffering for the resident could be resolved without pursuing MAID. The person's suffering was real, and we treated it with seriousness and dignity.

Late Snow, Amy

MARCH
WEEK 3

Metamorphosis Winging

metamorphosis winging
the searing shining raiment
(like "Raymond" to my young listening ear)
changed, shimmered
on Mountaintop dewdrop
refracting snowcap
crisp linen snapping
in eddies of updraft
like wings

and we shall be changed
from valley floor
where barns store
more bounty – so we build more silos
what for?
not our surplus but our very souls
are the goal of that shining shoal
Haven, playful respect for older Moses and Elijah
but so much more for Yeshua
"My Son" – listen.

Meditation - For Such a Time as This

Praying Psalm 44: We have heard it with our own ears, O God; our ancestors have told us what you did in their days. Not by weapons or terrorism or armies do you bring victory, but by your right hand, your arm, the light of your face and your love. We are brought down to the dust, our bodies cling to the ground. Rescue us because of your unfailing love.

Scripture Text - Esther 4:9-17
For if you remain silent at this time, relief and deliverance for the Jews will arise from another place, but you and your father's family will perish. And who knows but that you have come to your royal position for such a time as this? Esther 4:14

Each day every one of us has opportunities to make a difference. We may think that our influence is insignificant. We may be afraid to speak out when someone is being bullied or mistreated. We may ignore those inner promptings to give someone a call or text or email. And sometimes, there is some looming challenge or opposition where we need to take a stand in the face of evil.

Esther had such a challenge. For most of her life, this young woman had followed the direction and lead of others: her family, her appointed directors, and her husband, King Xerxes. Now she was called upon to be proactive. Passive behaviour now had to become active. She needed to take a stand. And she did. (Read the rest of the book of Esther.)

Is God giving you an opportunity today to become active? To stand up for what you know is right? To recognize that at this time, in this moment, in this situation, you are the right person to make a difference. God wants to use you – for such a time as this.

Suggested Song: "In Times Like These"

Pray: God of all power and vision, I ask for wisdom and strength on this day. As you call me to serve in my world, may I enter with the peace of Christ, the joy of the Spirit, and a calm dependence on You, my Heavenly Father. In Jesus' name, Amen.

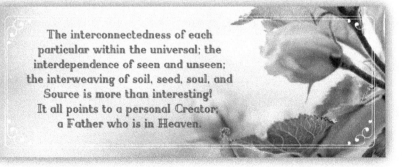

The interconnectedness of each particular within the universal; the interdependence of seen and unseen; the interweaving of soil, seed, soul, and Source is more than interesting! It all points to a personal Creator; a Father who is in Heaven.

Meditation - Everything is Beautiful

☀ **Praying Psalm 45:** My heart is stirred by your Word. Raise up a most excellent leader full of grace and your blessings. Beauty, wisdom, wealth, prosperity, and progeny are all gifts from you, Creator Father. Give us praiseworthy leaders in our land.

📖 **Scripture Text** - Ecclesiastes 3:1-11
He has made everything beautiful in its time. He has also set eternity in the human heart. Ecclesiastes 3:11

I have been involved in many memorial services. I have sung at funerals, spoken, prayed in services in churches, chapels and at gravesites. It is a deep and sincere privilege to come alongside families at times of such grief and challenge.

One of the texts I often share is this one from Ecclesiastes. A time for everything, the Preacher (*Qoheleth*) says, even death.

Unquestionably, there are many beautiful moments and experiences in life. A stunning sunrise or sunset, the crashing surf at the ocean, a calm, cool forest, the birth of a child, the wedding of a young couple. However, some of the things listed in Ecclesiastes 3 may not be so beautiful: a time to weep, a time to tear down, a time for war. Everything is beautiful? Really?

But the author says that "God has made everything beautiful."

Romans 8:28 says *"And we know that in all things God works for the good of those who love him, who have been called according to his purpose."* This verse is frequently misquoted to say all *things* work together for good... but remember, it says, "*God* works." The pain, sadness, tragedies of life can only be made beautiful by God's grace and in God's time.

🎵 **Suggested Song:** "When Peace Like A River"

🙏 **Pray:** Loving God, I choose to trust you in both the beautiful and painful things of life – for you are Lord of all, in Jesus' name I pray, Amen.

Meditation - Pray Like You Mean It

Praying Psalm 46: Lord, you have been my Refuge and Strength, a very present help in trouble. In you I have no fear, though the earth gives way. For you are God. I follow the course of the river whose stream makes me glad – your holy place – I will be still and know that you are God. I exalt You!

Scripture Text - Ecclesiastes 12:1-8
Remember your Creator – before the silver cord is severed, and the golden bowl is broken; before the pitcher is shattered at the spring, and the wheel broken at the well. Ecclesiastes 12:6

We were gathered for our church's weekly time of prayer when one of the regulars spoke a beautiful prayer of praise and worship. I sensed the warmth and sincerity of her words, so I glanced over to watch her as she prayed. I cannot fully describe it, but what I thought I saw was a silver beam of light from the top of her head ascending into the arches of the church ceiling. It was fleeting, indescribable, and powerful. Perhaps this is what the writer had in mind: "Remember your Creator – before the silver cord is severed."

The text is a reminder to focus on our Creator while we still have breath in our lungs, capacity and desire in our hearts, passion and will in our spirits. To focus on God.

It was only a few months after this beautiful prayer time that this elderly saint died. The "silver cord was severed."

Suggested Song: "Precious Lord, Take My Hand"

Pray: Heavenly Father, I want to pray like I mean it. Like I know you're listening. Like I am connected to you in my spirit. Thank you for the wonderful privilege of coming to you in prayer, in Jesus' name, Amen.

Gifts and Abilities

I was constantly amazed and moved by the variety and diversity of each resident's gifts and abilities. Helga had a beautiful singing voice even in her late eighties. Sally had an astounding memory for dates, numbers, and people's birthdays! Many residents displayed deep spirituality, reflecting a meaningful long-term relationship with their Friend Jesus. The stories of residents about their family homes, many on a farm or in small rural communities, were inspiring. Each person has their story. Sometimes it was hard to remember the details, but always worth the wait and patience to hear the telling. And the joy of hearing Helga sing, recalling lyrics of songs from long ago, "The More We Get Together – the Happier We'll Be." I would delight in quizzing Sally about a date or a staff member's birthday. She was amazing. They are all amazing!

Good Shepherd, Sarah

Good Shepherd

Like a shepherd lead me...
How am I best lead?
By directive, documents, policies,
procedures and protocol
or by gentle firm modeling
and warm footprints on soft dewy grass?

Much we need Thy tender care...
How do I best serve when I lead?
By edict, directive, text or phone
or by caring companioning and compassionate concern
guarding guiding?

Blessed Jesus, Thou hast bought us,
loved us, and now sitting at the right hand
Cosmic Christ, Good Shepherd, Thine we are.

Meditation: Among the Exiles

Praying Psalm: 47: I rejoice and celebrate in you. I clap my hands and shout to you with cries of joy. You are awesome. I sing Your praises. You reign over the nations, you are omnipotent; the leaders of the earth belong to you. I exalt you.

Scripture Text - Ezekiel 1:1-6, 15-18
In my thirtieth year, in the fourth month on the fifth day, while I was among the exiles by the Kebar River, the heavens were opened and I saw visions of God. Ezekiel 1:1

As I began my third year as chaplain at Tabor Village, our alphabetical reflections through the Bible took us to the book of Ezekiel. A huge book with complex passages, but I decided to reflect on its message for declining times. It was the end of the kingdom, of the temple, of freedom, and the chosen people were in exile. These are themes that sadly resonate with many older adults facing final days. But where could I find devotional hope?

Ezekiel was not alone. He was placed in a specific geographic location, at a precise time, with a chosen group of people (verse 1). While they were in exile, they were not without hope.

Whatever our age or stage of life, we can enter and walk through times of discouragement and even depression. Ezekiel and his colleagues were in distress, away from home and their familiar settings. (Sounds something like the experience of the residents I was speaking to.) Then God gave the prophet a vision! Be amazed, even in the maze of life.

Suggested Song: "Ezekiel Saw the Wheel"

Pray: Loving Father, I pray for a sense of your glory, of hope and truth. Thank you that even in dark times, you are the light of the world, in Jesus' name, Amen.

Renovation requires demolition.

Meditation - Come to Life

Praying Psalm 48: You are great, Lord, worthy of praise. Your beauty is seen in all you touch, earth, mountains, and your holy place, Mount Zion. I meditate on your unfailing love and praise your righteousness. Your judgments make me glad. You are God forever and ever; you guide, even to the end.

Scripture Text - Ezekiel 37:1-6
This is what the Sovereign LORD says to these bones: I will make breath enter you, and you will come to life. Ezekiel 37:5

Our high school choir used to sing the spiritual, "Dem Bones, Dem Bones, Dem Dry Bones," based on this text from the prophet Ezekiel. This energetic song is an expression of hope for the hopeless, life for the lifeless, breath for the breathless. The Sovereign Lord says, "I will make breath enter you." It is reminiscent of the account in Genesis where God breathes life into the lifeless form, and it becomes a living being (Genesis 2:7). We need God's breath, God's Holy Spirit in our lives.

In Hebrew and in Greek the words *ruah* and *pneuma* mean spirit, wind, breath. When Jesus spoke with Nicodemus about being born again by the Spirit, Jesus said, *"The wind blows wherever it pleases. You hear its sound, but you cannot tell where it comes from or where it is going. So it is with everyone born of the Spirit."* John 3:8

We all need God's energizing, life-giving breath. Come, Holy Spirit.

Suggested Song: "Spirit of God, Descend Upon My Heart"

Pray: Thank you, Holy Spirit, for your activity in my life today. I invite you to breathe fresh thoughts, creative vision, compassion for the lost, and a desire to love you, God, follow you, and serve you in Jesus' name, Amen.

Enter, Ray

Meditation - A Devoted Teacher

Praying Psalm 49: Grant me your wisdom, Lord, relating to wealth, hard times, pride, death, and decay. Redeem my life, father, allow me to share your loving plan with the perishing.

Scripture Text - Ezra 7:6-10
For Ezra had devoted himself to the study and observance of the Law of the LORD, and to teaching its decrees and laws in Israel. Ezra 7:10

I am very thankful and appreciative of the many devoted teachers I have had in my life. School teachers, university professors, and gifted Bible teachers. People who have devoted themselves in a particular discipline and have spent years learning and growing are an inspiration.

We are all called to be lifelong learners. We are followers of Jesus, his disciples, his lifelong students. Ezra had devoted himself to the study and observance of the law of the Lord. The law included the Ten Commandments, and all the instructions for living a full and flourishing life. Ezra was called by God to teach others in the community to love and obey God.

Our master teacher, Jesus, invites us to come, to learn from him, for his yoke is easy and his burden is light (Matthew 11:28). Not all of life's lessons are easy to learn. Ezra had some very difficult things to teach the people of God. What do you need to learn today? Go to Jesus, the Teacher.

Suggested Song: "O Master Let Me Walk With Thee"

Pray: Loving Heavenly Father, I thank you for the many people in my life who have devoted themselves to teaching me. I thank you for your living Word, the Bible, thank you that Jesus is the Master Teacher, and I invite you today to lead and teach me. In Jesus' name I pray, Amen.

Rejoice and Be Glad

Morning prayers at Tabor often included the scripture song "This Is the Day" (that the Lord has made, we will rejoice and be glad in it). (Psalm 118:24) Staff members would smile and sometimes clap along. I am sure that many of the residents did not feel joyful. Perhaps some were experiencing discomfort, others had a poor night's sleep and most had the ongoing challenge of restricted mobility and declining strength. But for these few moments, people could choose to rejoice in the gift of the day God had given.

In Letters Plain

"Mission" "Vision" "Values"
the writings on the wall
three words to guide community
by words we rise and fall.

MENE, TEKEL, PARSIN
number, weigh, divide
three words to make a heart stop
from words he couldn't hide.

"faith" "hope" and "charity"
these three things remain
the greatest is agape
Love, in letters plain.

Tabor Village – Mission, Vision, and Values – framed and hanging on the wall.
Daniel 5, 1 Corinthians 13

Meditation - A Healthy Hope

Praying Psalm 50: Lord, you shine out like the sun from rising to setting. Like a devouring fire, a raging tempest, a summoning sovereign. I listen to your instructions. I meditate on them. I choose to make my life a sacrifice of thank offerings to honour you.

Scripture Text - Galatians 3:6-9
So those who rely on faith are blessed along with Abraham, the man of faith. Galatians 3:9

When I shared this Galatians text in March 2018 at Tabor Home, the theme for the month was "Hope." It was also nutrition month. As we focused on good, healthy nutrition, I tried to encourage the community to embrace "healthy hope."

The text refers to Abraham as a person of faith. He believed God would be faithful to keep his promise even though Abraham's situation seemed increasingly hopeless. What a wonderful encouragement, then, to think of ourselves as the children of Abraham, because we have come to God through faith in Christ Jesus. The promise made to Abraham that all nations would be blessed through him, gives us motivation and desire to bless people around us each day.

As children, we sometimes sang a song called "Father Abraham." It wasn't very biblically nuanced, but it was fun! Maybe the point of that song was that God's blessing was poured out in history, is poured out in our lives today, and is available to be poured into the lives of the coming generations as well. May it be so.

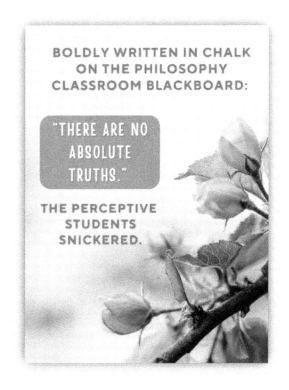

BOLDLY WRITTEN IN CHALK ON THE PHILOSOPHY CLASSROOM BLACKBOARD:

"THERE ARE NO ABSOLUTE TRUTHS."

THE PERCEPTIVE STUDENTS SNICKERED.

Suggested Song: "Make Me A Blessing"

Pray: Heavenly Father, Lord God of Abraham, thank you for your many promises. Thank you for fulfilling your promise to Abraham. You bless people through your wonderful fulfillment to bless the nations. Use me today to bless those around me. In Jesus' name I pray, Amen.

Meditation - Abba, Father

Praying Psalm 51: Have mercy on me, O God, because of your unfailing love. Because of your great compassion, blot out the stains of my sins. For I was born a sinner. Purify me from my sin and I will be clean; wash me and I will be whiter than snow. Restore to me the joy of your salvation; then I will teach your ways to rebels.

Scripture Text - Galatians 4:1-7

And because you are children, God has sent the Spirit of his Son into our hearts, crying, "Abba! Father!" Galatians 4:6

What a privilege it is to come to the creator of all things as a trusting child. Jesus taught us to pray, "Our Father, who is in heaven." Paul also reminds us that we are now children of God, living in the Spirit of his Son (verse 6), so we have the family rights to pray, "*Abba!* Father!"

Unfortunately, not everyone has had a healthy "father" model in their lives. The reference to "father" implies the perfect image of a loving, guarding, guiding parent. Obviously, no earthly father could ever be perfect, but God is a perfect Father. And we are not perfect children! But we have been transformed from slaves to children of God.

In the Greco-Roman world, a wealthy citizen would often employ a guardian to teach, watch, and guide the child as they approached maturity. Paul uses this image for the law of the scriptures. Instructing and preparing us to become full inheritors of the Kingdom of God through Jesus Christ.

What a privilege.

Suggested Song: "What A Friend We Have In Jesus"

Pray: Heavenly Father, *Abba*, thank you for inviting me to pray in such an intimate and personal way to you, my Creator, Sustainer, Redeemer. Help me to live as a trusting child today, in Jesus' name I pray, Amen.

Meditation - Very Good

Praying Psalm 52: Your justice continues forever. I want to thrive like an olive tree planted in your presence. I will praise you forever for what you have done.

Scripture Text - Genesis 1:27-31

God saw everything that he had made, and indeed, it was very good. And there was evening and there was morning, the sixth day. Genesis 1:31

When we hear an encouraging word and commendation from someone we love, it means so much. When we have spent hours working on a project and someone comes along and says, "That's very good," we are blessed.

Sometimes we are guilty of being overly critical of our own efforts. Perhaps we have been working in the garden, painting a picture, or building a fence. We can always see the flaws and imperfections. So, when God said in Genesis 1:27, "It was very good," it must indeed have been excellent!

God continues to work in this beautiful world. Yes, it is marred by sin, brokenness, imperfection, but it all started as an excellent expression of our Creator God. We need to remind ourselves that the creation culmination according to Genesis chapter 1 is humankind (verse 27). God created us in God's image, blessed us and provided all we need to flourish on this beautiful home planet.

Let's do our part to restore the beauty, through the good works we can do through Christ Jesus, *"For we are God's handiwork, created in Christ Jesus to do good works, which God prepared in advance for us to do."* Ephesians 2:10.

Suggested Song: "How Great Thou Art"

Pray: Father God, Creator of this beautiful world, I agree with you today – it is very good. Help me as I work in my small way to make it a better world in all I do and say. In Jesus' name, Amen.

I Want to Go Home

I heard many sad stories of childhood. Stories about fathers who never affirmed or encouraged their children, carried as a wound for seven or eight decades. Stories about the death of siblings, impacting the family in immeasurable, unimaginable ways. Some would tell stories about getting lost as a child, and the memory was so vivid and frightening that it loomed large in the present, and often included the frequent request, "I want to go home," sometimes asking for mommy and daddy. "You'll be home soon," I silently thought, and sometimes spoke. As staff, we are trained to redirect residents if they are agitated or becoming distressed. Redirecting a life story is something to be treated with respect, thoughtfulness, and care.

Seashore, Hudson

You Seemed to Save

Did you raise your voice
in anger above swirling desert winds?
Did your hunger fuel frustration
at meadows bereft of manna?
Did your interrogation with the Adversary
intrigue or aggravate – both You and him?

You seemed to save your anger:
      for leaders who led astray,
      for opponents of the way,
      for Temple clutter's rot display
      for death and Sin and putrid decay!

Meditation - Where Are You?

☀ **Praying Psalm 53:** I acknowledge you, O God, for I am no fool. I choose to turn towards you. Keep me doing right. I shout with joy because you rescue and restore.

📖 **Scripture Text** - Genesis 3:6-10
But the LORD God called to the man, "Where are you?" Genesis 3:9

Did God misplace Adam and Eve? Did the omnipotent, omniscient Creator need to ask the question, "Where are you?"

It is a relational question, not locational. Where are you in relationship to me? Why are you hiding? Tell me, what is going on in your heart? What does it feel like to be naked before our Creator?

We all have different strategies to try to hide: hide from others, hide from ourselves, hide from God. This is one of the results of disobedience, wilfulness, and sin.

So we need to ask ourselves each day, "Where am I in relationship to God?" "Where am I in relationship to others?"

Jesus was once asked, what is the most important commandment? He replied, *"'Love the Lord your God with all your heart and with all your soul and with all your mind.' This is the first and greatest commandment. And the second is like it: 'Love your neighbour as yourself.'"* (Matthew 22:37-39) To love God and others is to be in relationship. To stop hiding. To embrace and receive forgiveness, love, and reconciliation.

Where are you?

🎵 **Suggested Song:**
"Draw Me Nearer"

🙏 **Pray:** Loving God and Heavenly Father, I want to draw close to you today. Forgive me for my sins and for running away from you and trying in vain to hide from you and from myself. Fill me, Holy Spirit, with love for others, and may I live in deep relationship with Father, Son, and Holy Spirit, in Jesus' name, Amen.

Technique is the discipline which precedes the comment, "You make it seem so easy."

Meditation – Promise

Praying Psalm 54: Come with great power, O God, and rescue me. Listen to my prayer. Pay attention to my plea. You are my helper; you keep me alive! I will praise your name, O Lord, for it is good.

Scripture Text - Genesis 8:15-22
As long as the earth endures, seedtime and harvest, cold and heat, summer and winter, day and night will never cease. Genesis 8:22

The seasons give us clear markers and indications that the times are changing. Moving from winter to spring with the promise of hope and fresh flowers and blooming trees is a time of encouragement. As spring moves into summer and the warmer, longer days, we celebrate the beauty of creation and enjoy times of recreation. Then moving into autumn, for many of us this is a time to start back to school, to keep learning and to enjoy harvest. Then the cycle repeats as we move back into winter, dormancy, quiet, reflection.

In our text, the promise of God's love and faithfulness is expressed in beautiful poetic form depicting the cycle of the seasons. Sometimes the seasons of our life challenge our faith. Noah had been through an extreme time of testing. He had endured criticism, ridicule, uncertainty, hard work, and terror. Through it all, God promised to be faithful.

Whatever you may be going through in this season of your life, be assured that God is faithful. When I shared this devotion with Tabor Home residents in March 2018, each one of them was experiencing different reactions and emotions in their season of life. I reminded them that spring in the beautiful Fraser Valley was just around the corner.

Suggested Song: "Great Is Thy Faithfulness"

Pray: Loving Heavenly Father, I thank you for your faithfulness through the seasons of my life. You are with me even in challenging times. Thank you for the vitality of springtime, the warmth of summer, the flourishing of autumn, and the beauty of winter. I praise you, in Jesus' name, Amen.

Meditation - Silent in the Storm

Praying Psalm 55: Listen to my prayer, O God, do not ignore my cry for help! My enemies shout at me, making loud and wicked threats. My heart pounds in my chest. The terror of death assaults me. O that I had wings like a dove; then I would fly far away to the quiet of the wilderness.

Scripture Text - Habakkuk 2:20–3:2
The LORD is in his holy temple; let all the earth be silent before him. Habakkuk 2:20

Many of us have experienced the calm before the storm. Both in nature and in our life. That eerie sense of silent anticipation. Awe mixed with fear. The people in Habakkuk's time had experienced a storm in their political, social, religious life. And there was more stormy weather ahead.

The prophet Habakkuk cries out, "How long, Lord, must I call for help, but you do not listen?" (1:2) People in our day are crying out with the same prayer. How long before You help me, God? Maybe God wants to use us to help them with their cry for help. In whatever way we can reach out to those around us, may we have our eyes open, and our hearts sensitized to the needs of others.

In the storms of life, when we cry out, God hears. God may choose to respond immediately with a "Yes." Sometimes the answer is "Not yet." Sometimes, God says "No." It is difficult to accept "No" as an answer. God is present. God is sovereign. God is in his holy temple. Let us learn how to keep silent before our powerful, awesome God.

Suggested Song: "A Shelter in the Time of Storm"

Pray: O Lord, my God, I wait in silence before you (pause).
In the silence, receive my trusting worship. Thank you for hearing me, in Jesus' name, Amen.

God's Amazing Love

Spiritual battles are very common and can be extremely intense at the end of life. A person may have become a Christian years ago and faithfully walked with God for decades, but the enemy continues to pursue and persist. Alice was clearly concerned as she shared, "I feel like I'm no good, I can't be saved, I'll never get to heaven." When I asked her what she was experiencing, and the nature of the attack, even the simple, profound act of calling it an "enemy attack" brought some relief. We talked about God's amazing love, to send Jesus to forgive our sins and give us new life. I shared scripture and prayed for release from the attack, for strength to overcome this relentless attack of the enemy of our souls.

Sea Fever, Ralph

Holy Week - An Unholy Mess

What an unholy mess
We're made of things.
Pious words and postures
Impious expressions of division
Gloating over a sham victory
in which no one wins
no one can win.

As Jesus cleared the temple
entering the centre
of religious hucksterism
clear our local church:
      drive out the pride
      whip our sorry selfish backs
      overturn tables of business as usual.

We need a cleansing
Wind of the Spirit
create us new hearts:
      Where there is stubborn pride –
      Compliance and trust
      Where there is self-centred righteousness
      Your peace – pass the shalom
How have we become an unholy market?
What can we do to recover holy zeal?
When will we know true cleansing?
How have I, a religious leader, become unreal?

Meditation - Voices for Our Times

Praying Psalm 56: Be merciful to me, my God, for my enemies are in hot pursuit; when I am afraid, I put my trust in you. I am under vows to you, my God. I will present my thank offerings to you.

Scripture Text - Haggai 1:12-15

Then Haggai, the LORD's messenger, gave this message of the LORD to the people: "I am with you," declares the LORD. Haggai 1:13

A prophet speaks because God has told them to. Biblical prophets obeyed God's call to speak God's message to the people. Regardless of their personal popularity or the reception of the message, they spoke with boldness, courage, imagination, and inspiration. The prophet Haggai was no exception. His word to the people of his day echoes down the centuries to our own time: "'I am with you,' declares the Lord."

We each might have different suggestions as to who is the voice of our time. Some might say Martin Luther King Junior, others may point to Nelson Mandela, or Billy Graham. Haggai was a voice for his time.

Who are we listening to these days? With the prevalence of media, entertainment, popular trends, and fads, we are overwhelmed with voices.

The prophets, including John the Baptist, point us to God in the wilderness saying, *"Look, the Lamb of God, who takes away the sins of the world."* (John 1:29) Today, let us recommit to listening to the voice of Jesus.

Suggested Song: "Jesus Calls Us"

Pray: Lord Jesus, thank you for saving me, for forgiving my sin, and giving me new life – eternal life. With all the voices around me today, I choose to listen to You. In your name I pray, Amen.

THE GLIDING SWAN ON A CALM LAKE; ONLY LOOK BENEATH THE SURFACE TO SEE THE VIGOROUS MOTION.

Meditation - Hold Firmly

Psalm 57: Have mercy on me, my God, have mercy on me, for in you I take refuge. I will take refuge in the shelter of your wings until the disaster has passed. Be exalted, O God, above the heavens, let your glory be over all the earth.

Scripture Text - Hebrews 4:14-16
Therefore, since we have a great high priest who has ascended into heaven, Jesus the Son of God, let us hold firmly to the faith we profess. Hebrews 4:14

It is always interesting to hear stories about your family and heritage. Sometimes as children we got bored listening to an older adult in our family telling the same stories over and over. However, as we get older ourselves, we realize the precious opportunities those stories afford to connect to our past, our roots, our personal family history.

The scriptures teach us that we are part of a much larger family, the family of faith. We have in Jesus the perfect high priest, pointing the way to heaven, and we are invited to stand firmly in our faith. When we know our past, we have context for our present, and renewed hope for the future. When faced with challenges, we know we have one who has gone before us, leading, and guiding us as the Good Shepherd. Let us hold firmly to the faith we profess.

Suggested Song:
"My Hope is Built"

Pray: Our Heavenly Father, thank you for the family of God of which we are a part. Like any family, we confess we are imperfect, and we need you to be our firm hope. Today I thank you and pray for a deeper faith in you, and a greater confidence to share that faith with others, in Jesus' name, Amen.

Flourish, Ray

Meditation – Pioneer

Praying Psalm 58: O Lord, bring justice to our land, the rulers, leaders, lawyers, and judges. Judge the unjust, O God. Reward the righteous. You are the God who judges the earth.

Scripture Text - Hebrews 12:1-3

Fixing our eyes on Jesus, the pioneer and perfecter of faith. For the joy set before him he endured the cross, scorning its shame, and sat down at the right hand of the throne of God. Hebrews 12:2

Pioneers are hardy folk. They are sometimes eccentric, always visionary, deeply courageous, and optimistic. To pioneer any new initiative, or travel to a different location, or introduce new methods and ideas, is to put yourself in a position of possible rejection and ridicule. But it also puts you in a position to be a leader.

When we acknowledge Jesus as our pioneer, we are affirming that he has set a new direction, and we are willing to follow his lead. Some translations of this text use the word "author" instead of "pioneer." An author creates new stories, new possibilities, adventure, and direction. If Jesus is the author of our life-story, we are open to experiencing and living the plot and purpose he desires. In a true sense, Jesus has "authority" in our lives because he was willing to go before us, and even endure the cross to provide our salvation.

Suggested Song: "Precious Lord, Take My Hand"

Pray: Loving God, thank you for sending Jesus into this world to be our perfect pioneer. I ask for strength today to fix my eyes on Jesus, to continue to walk with him, talk with him, learn from him, and pray in his name, Amen.

Proof Enough

We were talking about prayer. I asked Lorraine if she prayed. She told me her story about being alone on the farm as a young girl, her parents were in town, and a calf got caught in the fencing. She was too small to help the calf get free, so she prayed "Lord, please save this calf." Just then the calf twisted and released itself. For Lorraine, this was proof enough! So, whenever we met, after some conversation and singing a hymn or song together, we would pray. She had faith. We usually try to fix things on our own, but Lorraine knew immediately that she needed to pray. She still does.

Donkey Song

I had never carried a load before
So his weight on my back seemed odd.
The two men who came to my stall that day
Didn't need to push or prod;
It was all arranged with a word or two
There was talk of a prophet of God.
I was led from the barn through the village street
On hard pavement instead of green sod.
I had never carried a load before
But his weight on my back seemed light.
Some garments were laid on me, then he sat,
I felt no panic or fright.
Instead, I sensed calm and a peaceful command
As the crowds pressed in close, left and right.
For a colt from the village with a sheltered life
I was unprepared for the sight.

The crowd had taken their coats and cloaks
And laid them out on the road.
My footsteps were softened by the clothes on the path,
In the distance Jerusalem glowed.
The city was stirred, all were shouting "God Save"
"Hosanna" Their praises flowed . . .
The weight on my back seemed to grow step by step
As He waited to bear His own load.

Meditation - Come Back To Me

Praying Psalm 59: Deliver me from my enemies, O God, be my fortress against those who are attacking me. You are my strength; I sing praises to you. God, you are my fortress, my God on whom I can rely.

Scripture Text - Hosea 14:1-6
Take words with you and return to the LORD. Say to him: "Forgive all our sins and receive us graciously, that we may offer the fruit of our lips." Hosea 14:2

Some people lead incredibly difficult lives. We all have challenges and difficulties in life from time to time. Then there are people who seem to be in constant turmoil. A person like that in the biblical tradition is the prophet Hosea. What an unusual and even bizarre calling God placed on his life. God directed this faithful servant to live a life of brokenness and relational tragedy (Hosea 1:2).

God was not punishing Hosea for any personal sin or transgression. God felt Hosea was strong enough and worthy to bear the load of repeatedly being betrayed by his wife Gomer (3:1). God was using Hosea to dramatically convey to the people God loved, "Come back to me."

I am sure that people look at Hosea with judgmental and critical hearts. He bore that. Perhaps there were other people who felt sympathy for Hosea, urging him to forget about trying to reconcile with his wife. "A lost cause," they might have told him.

A lost cause, humanity. Yet Jesus bore the load for our sins. To demonstrate the loving call, "Come back."

Suggested Song: "The Love of God"

Pray: Lord, today I pray for those who are living difficult lives. If these difficulties are due to disobedience and poor decisions, may they hear your call today: "Come back to me." And Lord, I confess that I wander and wonder – draw me to yourself – heal my waywardness. In Jesus' name, Amen.

Home, family, healthy relationships, love, service to others:

good roots produce good fruits.

Meditation - Joy Draws a Crowd

Praying Psalm 60: You have rejected us, God, and burst upon us. You have been angry with us – now restore us! God has spoken from his sanctuary in triumph. With God, we will gain the victory.

Scripture Text - Isaiah 49:8-13

Shout for joy, you heavens; rejoice, you earth; burst into song, you mountains! For the LORD comforts his people and will have compassion on his afflicted ones. Isaiah 49:13

In the month of May 2018, our daily devotional theme at Tabor Home was "Joy." Now, many of the residents, families, and staff, were experiencing the challenges of life in a care home. Where is the joy, some might ask? And yet, every day in conversation with people, we would find things in our lives to be joyful about. For some, it was the warmth of the spring sunshine. For others it was a loved one visiting and reading a story. Each had a different cause for joy.

Isaiah reminds us that the Lord comforts us. And with that comfort we can be filled with joy. The apostle Paul knew hardships that are beyond most of our imaginings: imprisonment, beatings, shipwreck, and he was able to express and encourage others to experience great joy.

Philippians 4:4: *"Rejoice in the Lord always. I will say it again: Rejoice!"*

Joy draws a crowd. (Isaiah 49:12)

Suggested Song: "The Joy of the Lord is My Strength"

Pray: Loving Heavenly Father, I thank you for the joy you place within my heart today. As I share that joy with others, may people be drawn to you, rejoice and be comforted. In Jesus' name, Amen.

Flowing Stream, Leona

Meditation - A Timely Text

Praying Psalm 61: O God, listen to my cry! Hear my prayer! From the ends of the earth, I cry to you for help when my heart is overwhelmed. Lead me to the Rock that is higher than I.

Scripture Text - Isaiah 61:1-3
The Spirit of the Sovereign LORD is on me, because the LORD has anointed me to proclaim good news to the poor. He has sent me to bind up the brokenhearted, to proclaim freedom for the captives and release from darkness for the prisoners. Isaiah 61:1

Word about Jesus was spreading. People were hearing about the miracles, about his storytelling, about his compassion. So, when he arrived in the synagogue in his hometown of Nazareth that Sabbath day, and was handed the scroll, he read Isaiah 61 (Luke 4:17-21).

Maybe the rabbi in charge was just being courteous to this homegrown young man as he handed him the scroll of Isaiah. Maybe that was the appointed reading for the day. It was certainly the appointed text for the time. Jesus was indeed fulfilling the promise of the prophet Isaiah. Jesus was full of the Holy Spirit (Luke 4:1). Good news was being proclaimed. Freedom and recovery were the new order of the day.

The living word was being fulfilled by the Living Word. This text is timely for us.

We all need good news. Who doesn't want to live with open eyes and an open heart? How many who mourn need to be comforted today?

Suggested Song: "Wonderful Words of Life"

Pray: Heavenly Father, your word is perfect. Today we need to hear your Word in a fresh, applicable way. Help us to live out the truth we know and seek strength to be faithful in proclaiming your good news today, in Jesus' name, Amen.

God is SO GOOD

Some residents are very withdrawn, seeming to disengage with everything and everyone around them. Julie was like this. Eyes closed, head dropped on her chest, not participating in any attempts to include her. But when I brought my guitar into the room and started to sing "God is So Good," Julie would gradually lift her head and open her eyes, joining exuberantly in "God is SO GOOD!" She almost shouted it. Where was she when we tried all the other methods of engagement? In some deep, inner, quiet, private space. But suddenly, seemingly overcome by the love and goodness of God, Julie reaffirmed life's central reality: God is SO GOOD.

MAY
WEEK 1

Praying Psalm 62: Truly my soul finds rest in you O God, my salvation comes from you. Lord, both the lowly and the privileged are only a breath. I don't set my heart on stolen goods. Power belongs to you O God, with you is unfailing love.

Still Moving

I can't get a deep breath!
I can't breathe. I can't get I can't
     "Your old men will dream dreams"
old man's 'best friend' *pneumonia*
breath seizer, breath cease-er
wind, water, fluids and flux
phlegm: a temperament of stolid,
solemnity – also membranes
mucus saturated – dream of going over
taking the freshest deepest breath.

Hard labour – breathing exploring
mini deaths between each
rib and exhale; shallow, pale
     "old men ought to be explorers"
old men aught, caught, taught,
taut teeter on newness up-and-down
leverage of communion,
cleaving skies, leaving lies still and still moving.

Meditation - All My Trials, Lord

Praying Psalm 63: You, God, are my God, earnestly I seek you. I thirst for you, my whole being longs for you. I have seen you in the sanctuary and witnessed your power and glory. On my bed I remember you. I think of you through the watches of the night.

Scripture Text - James 1:2-5

Consider it pure joy, my brothers and sisters, whenever you face trials of many kinds. James 1:2

How can trials be a joy? Several years ago, I visited a person in hospital who was seriously ill. As we talked, I felt prompted to read this text from James to this friend in a hospital bed. I was a bit uneasy reading these words to someone who was suffering. But I also felt deeply convicted that they were the words this person needed to hear.

Years later, after this patient had fully recovered, we had a conversation about that hospital visit. My friend shared that these words, *"Consider it pure joy, my brothers and sisters, whenever you face trials of many kinds,"* gave hope, confidence, and peace. I learned several things from that experience. The first was to listen to the inner promptings of the Holy Spirit. The second was a reaffirmation of the power of the Word of God. A third lesson was that trials and challenges can be a portal to peace, and a journey towards joy.

Suggested Song: "Take My Hand, Precious Lord"

Pray: Loving God, you are the Source of all joy, peace, and comfort. Many today are facing the trials of being persecuted for their faith in Jesus. Grant them perseverance, courage, and character. Give us compassion and wisdom as we come alongside those who are suffering and facing trials. In Jesus' name, Amen.

The capital "E" Epiphany is echoed by countless, daily epiphanies.

Meditation - Count to Ten

Praying Psalm 64: Hear me, my God, as I voice my complaint; protect my life from the threats of the enemy. Hide me from the conspiracy of the wicked. Surely the human heart and mind are cunning. I rejoice in you, Lord, and take refuge in you. Receive my praise from an upright heart.

Scripture Text - James 3:3-12
With the tongue we praise our Lord and Father, and with it we curse human beings, who have been made in God's likeness. My brothers and sisters, this should not be. James 3:9-10

Were you ever encouraged as a child, when you felt the urge to say or do something angry or inappropriate, "Count to ten!" Sometimes, this simple method of pausing, reflecting, and evaluating before we speak can avoid much pain and hurt.

Another thing we were told when we were young that is simply not true is, "Sticks and stones may break my bones, but names will never hurt me." It is an attempt to guard ourselves from deep hurt that comes with cruel words. How much better to count to ten and allow words to bring healing, hope and help?

Today's text gives us three metaphors for the power of our tongue: a bit in the mouth of a horse, a ship's rudder, and a spark of flame in a dry forest. All three are small things that can wield great power and influence. Used correctly, our words can heal, praise, and encourage; used in anger they can crush. So, when it comes to hurtful words, James summarizes, *"My brothers and sisters, this should not be."*

Suggested Song: "Make Me A Blessing"

Pray: Loving Lord Jesus, please help me to guard my tongue today. May this powerful tool be used to bless, not crush. In Jesus' name I pray, Amen.

Glow, Ray

Meditation - In Good Hands

Praying Psalm 65: Praise awaits you in Zion, I worship you. You answered prayer with awesome and righteous deeds, God my Saviour, the hope of all the ends of the earth. You care for the land.

Scripture Text - Jeremiah 18:1-10
Can I not do with you, Israel, as this potter does?" declares the LORD. "Like clay in the hand of the potter, so are you in my hand, Israel. Jeremiah 18:6

When I was in high school, I had a very good art teacher. One of the outstanding things about his program was the pottery studio. We had the opportunity to learn how to mould clay, throw pottery, glaze, and bake the ceramics in kilns. Everyone in my family had pottery that I had made during Grades 11 and 12. How many sugar bowls does one family need?

The image of a potter shaping the clay is used by Jeremiah to remind us of God's sovereign grace in the lives of nations and individuals. Sometimes being shaped is painful. Sometimes we resist and wish our lives would look different. But our text reminds us that God is the Master Craftsman. The Maker. In God's hands, we are shaped and formed into the people who can obediently serve God and love others.

The apostle Paul also uses the metaphor of everyday jars of clay to indicate our call to simply serve, and serve simply (2 Corinthians 4:7). Humbling.

Suggested Song: "Have Thine Own Way, Lord"

Pray: Lord, again this day I choose to offer you my life, to be open to your shaping and forming hand. As I look at the world around me, I choose by faith to believe you are still the Master Potter, shaping nations as you see fit. In Jesus' name I pray, Amen.

Sacred Ground

Tabor has great staff. Each person brings their unique gifts and personalities to work with these folk whom they come to love and care for. It is not an easy job. In fact, it is more than a job, it is a calling. When I see the tenderness of Corina painting the fingernails of Heather, or Sue the housekeeper having a good laugh with Henry, or see Simi, a nurse, getting Carl up on his feet to dance to my guitar music, I often think – this is sacred ground. The simple acts of mercy, grace and human goodness reflect a much deeper, wider, all-encompassing love and care for each child of God. What a privilege to journey together.

Miraculous Manifestation: Instantaneous Fermentation!

Wine on the way,
Six stone water jars
Filled to the brim,
Not for wedding wine they are now repurposed.
And we do as we're told, "listen to him."

No ceremonial washing
On this third day celebration
Guests were there, food to spare
But now a tribulation – depleted libation!
Beyond imagination – a host's humiliation.

We drew the fresh pure water
Fearfully shuffled to the master
Of the banquet; we- the lowly waiters
His lips were moist with rich red wine
No blows, berating – all seemed fine
Because we followed orders
Do as He says; celebration divine.

Now every fall when I walk through
Vineyard; vines laden with wine on the way
I remember instantaneous transformation
Momentary fermentation - Vine displaying Sign.

Meditation - On My Mind

Praying Psalm 66: I take great joy in you, God, along with all the earth. How awesome are your deeds! So great is your power. Help me see more of what you have done, are doing! I give all my life to you as an offering. I praise you, God; you have not rejected my prayer or withheld your love from me.

Scripture Text - Jeremiah 31:31-34

This is the covenant I will make with the people of Israel after that time," declares the LORD. "I will put my law in their minds and write it on their hearts. I will be their God, and they will be my people. Jeremiah 31:33

"You've been on my mind recently." We sometimes speak these words to someone we haven't seen or talked with for some time. I believe that when someone comes to mind, it is the Spirit's way of prompting us to reach out to them. Maybe phone, email, text or write a letter or card. God says in Jeremiah, "*I will put my law in their minds.*"

The Bible needs to be constantly percolating, marinating, maturing in our mind. The Holy Spirit uses the Word of God to encourage, challenge, prompt and instruct us. We need to spend time in the Word regularly to let it have its full impact. Just as you are doing right now.

Jesus told us, in his Sermon on the Mount, that if we hear the words and don't put them into practice, our life is on shaky ground. (Matthew 7:26)

What's on your mind today?

Suggested Song: "Trust and Obey"

Pray: Loving God, thank you for your Word. As I read scripture today, may your voice speak to me in new and powerful ways. As you place your teaching in my mind today, may I live it out by the strength of your Holy Spirit. In Jesus' name, Amen.

time is a gift not a commodity.

Meditation – Praise

Praying Psalm 67: May you be gracious to us, God, and bless us and make your face shine on us, so that your way may be known on earth, your salvation among all nations. The land yields its harvest. God, you bless us still, we reverence/fear You.

Scripture Text - Job 1:13-22

Naked I came from my mother's womb, and naked I will depart. The LORD gave and the LORD has taken away; may the name of the LORD be praised. Job 1:21

How can we praise God when our life falls apart?

It is much easier to pray, to sing, to rejoice, when the blessings of life are abundant. But when we walk through dark valleys, what gives us cause to praise God?

The opening chapter of the book of Job is shocking. Yet, for many people in our world today, they are enduring shocking life-realities.

People who are being forced to flee their country as refugees.

People experiencing racism and hatred.

People who lost everything because of wildfires.

Maybe you have experienced this kind of devastation.

What can we learn from Job?

He begins by acknowledging his mortality and weakness. He also recognizes that everything he has and everything he enjoys is a gift from God. This dual posture of humility and gratitude led to an outburst of spontaneous praise, "May the name of the Lord be praised!"

Nothing in his human situation had changed. He was still bereft of his possessions and children. And he praised God. The chapter ends with these amazing words, *"In all this, Job did not sin by charging God with wrongdoing"* (verse 22).

Suggested Song: "Blessed Be The Name"

Pray: O God, in times of anguish and pain our first response is often withdrawal or anger. May I learn today from Job. May my life-response be humility, gratitude and praise. In Jesus' name, Amen.

Meditation - Tone of The Voice

Praying Psalm 68: Arise, O God, scatter Your enemies, blow them away like smoke. I sing to you and praise your name. I extol you who rides on the clouds. You are a good Father, Defender, Shelter.

Scripture Text - Job 38:1-7

Where were you ... while the morning stars sang together and all the angels shouted for joy? Job 38:7

The only answer Job could give to God's searing, searching question would be, "Absent."

This text makes me recollect two aspects of childhood. The first is the classroom roll call. Our names would be called alphabetically by the teacher, to which we dutifully replied, "Present." If there was silence, the inevitable conclusion was that student's absence – or else they weren't paying attention.

Job was not present when God laid the earth's foundations (verse 4), nor when the astronomical dimensions were set (verse 5), nor when the glory of the heavens broke into chorus (verse 7). Job was absent. So were we. So, best to remain silent.

The second childhood reflection is the expression, "Pick on someone your own size." Is God being a cosmic bully in this case? Some see it that way.

One paraphrase of God's opening statement to Job is, "Pull yourself together, Job! Up on your feet! Stand tall!" (verse 3 - *The Message,* by Eugene Peterson) My paraphrase might be, "Buckle your seatbelt, Job, get ready for a wild ride!" The experience was more amazement than an ambush. It's all in the tone of Voice.

Suggested Song: "How Great Thou Art"

Pray: Creator God and loving Heavenly Father, we are present with Job in confessing our absence when you performed your astonishing wonders. We are silenced in awe and worship of you. Wow! Thank you. In Jesus' name, Amen.

Good Stuff

At Tabor Village we have had many pastors as residents. Many of these church leaders had been pillars in the faith community for decades. God used these disciples of Jesus to lead people into deep relationship with God, and to form communities of faith throughout Canada and beyond. Pastor Arnie had a huge reputation in Abbotsford, so I often wondered what he received from my meditations on God's Word, our prayers, and songs together in our afternoon sessions. It was hard to communicate with Arnie, but one day after a session as I was visiting, he was trying to tell me something. As I leaned closer to hear, he softly said, "Good stuff."

Blossom, Amy

Notre Dame Fire: April 16, 2019

Shock and unspeakable grief
flickered on fire-lit faces
watching "Our Lady" burn.
Questions and disbelief
clouded, shrouded the darkened acrid air.

So much lost
treasures buried in ash debris
Holy Week marred by inferno,
melted crucifix and stained glass.

Yesterday - urgent, persistent fire response
seemed so little, desolate,
Today - serious investigation asking what, how, why?
Tomorrow - opening hearts and minds to what will arise.

And as the embers of Empire
Christendom die
What new birth awaits
Resurrection?

Meditation - If With All Your Hearts

Praying Psalm 69: Save me, O God, for the waters have come up to my neck. I sink, I descend into the deep waters, the floods engulf me. I am worn out calling for help, my eyes fail, looking for you. Answer me, Lord, out of the goodness of your love, in your great mercy turn to me, for I am in trouble. You hear the needy. Heaven and earth praise you; God will save.

Scripture Text - Joel 2:12-13
Return to the LORD your God, for he is gracious and compassionate, slow to anger and abounding in love. Joel 2:13

The nineteenth-century composer Felix Mendelssohn set this text dramatically in his oratorio *Elijah*. "Ye people, rend your hearts and not your garments!" The prophet Joel is calling people to true, heartfelt repentance and response to God, not merely outward show. So did the prophet Elijah. And so do preachers and teachers today.

I have had the privilege of singing this tenor recitative and the aria that follows in several performances of this great work. After several massive choruses with voices and orchestra thundering and soaring in polyphonic splendour, this recitative and aria shine like a gem. I loved singing it for its dramatic and declamatory impact, not least of which because it is followed by flowing words, "If with all your hearts ye truly seek me ... ye shall ever surely find me."

The prophets Joel and Elijah, the composer Mendelssohn, and other voices today are still calling us to return, for God is gracious and compassionate, slow to anger and abounding in love.

Suggested Song:
"Father, We Adore You"

Pray: Thank you, God, for your compassionate love and mercy. Today I turn to you with gratitude, awe, and the desire to see you more clearly, love you more dearly, follow you more nearly. In Jesus' name, Amen.

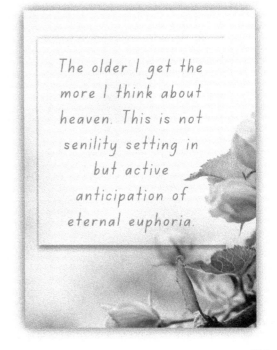

The older I get the more I think about heaven. This is not senility setting in but active anticipation of eternal euphoria.

Meditation - Dark Days

Praying Psalm 70: May all who seek you rejoice and be glad in you. May those who long for your saving help always say, "The Lord is great!" As for me, I am poor and needy, come quickly, O God, do not delay.

Scripture Text - 1 John 1:5-10
This is the message we have heard from him and declare to you: God is light; in him there is no darkness at all. 1 John 1:5

We are living in dark days. Climate change, extreme weather patterns, hatred, racism, pandemics. Many are struggling with discouragement and depression. You would almost think the letter we are reading from the apostle John to his brothers and sisters in Christ was written today. Yet we know it was written almost two thousand years ago. He speaks of darkness. Darkness represents ignorance, fear, doubt, and despair. When we try to walk in the dark, it can end badly. It can end in a fall.

When I shared this text with the folks at Tabor Home on February 9, 2020, none of us knew that we were days away from COVID-19 and worldwide pandemic. Talk about a period of darkness, despair, fear! Words like "God is light" and "in him is no darkness at all," although written centuries ago, are timeless and true. We have heard the message. Walk in the light.

Suggested Song: "The Light of the World Is Jesus"

Pray: Lord Jesus, I acknowledge that you are the light of the world. Give me courage to let my light shine in the darkness. I pray for those who are discouraged, fearful, depressed. May the light of Your joy illumine them right now, in Jesus' name I pray, Amen.

Meditation - Great Joy

Praying Psalm 71: In you, Lord, I have taken refuge, let me never be ashamed. In your righteousness, rescue me and deliver me, turn your ear to me and save me. Do not cast me away when I am old, do not forsake me when my strength is gone ... till I declare your power to the next generation, your mighty acts to all who are to come.

Scripture Text - 2 John 3-6
It has given me great joy to find some of your children walking in the truth, just as the Father commanded us. 2 John 4

Letter-writing is almost a lost art. There are still some individuals who write personal, longhand letters, but they are few and far between nowadays. With current technology, including email, texts, social media and telephone, letter-writing seems so old-fashioned.

It surprises some people to learn that letter-writing in the first century was a relatively new technology. Certainly, the writing of letters in pre-Christian times existed, but we are blessed in the Church to have these precious correspondences preserved and passed on to us. The reliability and efficiency of Roman roads and the *Pax Romana* made John's communication to his brothers and sisters in Christ a successful technology.

He said he had great joy to hear about believers walking in the truth. He expressed this joy in his letters. When was the last time you sent someone an encouraging letter? It could bring someone great joy.

Suggested Song: "I've Got the Joy - Down in My Heart"

Pray: Lord God, I thank you for my brothers and sisters in Christ today. As they read your Word, may they experience true joy and live in true faith. Help me today to reach out to someone and encourage them, maybe even send someone a letter. Use me today for your glory, Jesus, Amen.

Please Don't Give Up On Us

Affirmation can come in many ways. There are the public expressions of thanks and recognition which are sometimes awkward to receive, but truly appreciated. Then there are the kind notes and cards of thanks and encouragement, which I keep and sometimes reread on a difficult day. Also, the casual comments, phone calls or texts that would include an uplifting word. Sometimes affirmation can be bittersweet. One day, Ben and I were visiting, and he was sharing some thoughts and concerns with me. He stopped what he was saying, looked right at me and said, "Don't give up on us; please don't give up on us." I received it as acknowledgment that, whatever it was that I was doing was being appreciated, but it also contained a plaintive, sad tinge. Bittersweet.

Morning Coffees, Amy

Any Goliath Out There?

Any Goliath out there?
The echoed question reverberates
back from rocky hills
and dusty planes.

Of course, there are many
giants in the land
defying God, challenging his people.
Champions of opposition:
... daunting in stature
glistening bronze helmet
the latest technology and weaponry.

Five smooth stones
stripped of ill fitting, borrowed armor;
it only took one stream-sheened stone
forehead-embedded
and a ruddy confidence in the Name
(and some previous positive outcomes with
bear and lion encounters)

Against all odds, gods and taunting clods
 the victory came to the shepherd
boy – of almost ridiculous pedigree.

What of you and me? Any Goliath out there?

(1 Samuel 17)

Meditation - Consider Yourself at Home

Praying Psalm 72: Lord, give a heart of justice to our leaders. Prime ministers, presidents, monarchs, leaders in business and education, provincial, municipal, and civic leadership. Bring prosperity, help the poor and oppressed, extend the influence of a just leader from sea to sea.

Scripture Text - 3 John 5-8
We ought therefore to show hospitality to such people so that we may work together for the truth. 3 John 8

The term, "hospitality industry," is interesting. Sharing hospitality used to be a household demonstrating acceptance, generosity, and a cordial attitude towards others, very often to strangers. Today it has become an industry. There are many understandable reasons for this change, but Christians are still called to show hospitality. Travelling Christian in the first century relied on the love, kindness, and dignity shared in the very practical expression of a safe place to rest and be refreshed. I have often experienced warm reception and even accommodation in people's homes when I used to travel as a singer. They didn't know me, but they treated me like family. In a way, a care home is a place of hospitality. As we try to live out our love for God and love for people, as the commandment says, our expressions of support, nurture, and genuine grace is a way to honour God (verse 6). How does hospitality express itself in your life?

Suggested Song: "Blest Be the Tie That Binds"

Pray: Loving Father, thank you for the beautiful gift of hospitality. Help me to find creative and God-honouring ways to open myself and my homes to demonstrate love for others. Bless me as I seek ways to do this, in Jesus' name, Amen.

If you find yourself thinking "there's got to be more," that's because there is.

Meditation - Pure Nard

Praying Psalm 73: God, you are good to your people, to those who are pure in heart. Forgive any envy and wickedness. Guide me with your counsel and afterwards take me into glory.

Scripture Text - John 12:1-8
"Leave her alone," Jesus replied. "It was intended that she should save this perfume for the day of my burial." John 12:7

What do you give to someone who has everything? This is commonly asked when trying to choose a gift for someone who can afford to buy anything they need to provide for themselves; all their needs and more.

What can we give to Jesus, King of the Universe?

Mary poured pure nard, an expensive perfume for which she had spent perhaps her entire savings. Costly sacrifice.

When Judas Iscariot criticized this lavish waste, Jesus replied by saying two astounding things. He sharply rebuked his disciple, "Leave her alone." Jesus meant business. And he affirmed Mary's gesture as a premonition of Jesus' death and burial. Jesus meant business.

What can we give Jesus? The simple song expresses it this way:
"What can I give Him, poor as I am?
If I were a shepherd, I would bring Him a lamb.
If I were a wise man, I would do my part;
Yet what can I give Him? I give Him my heart."
Jesus, the holy one who meant business, wants no more – no less.

Suggested Song: "Just as I Am"

Pray: Loving God, thank you for sending your son, the Lord Jesus, to take away the sins of the world. Thank you for forgiving me. Today I offer my gift to you, in Jesus' name, Amen.

Meditation - Yes, Lord

Praying Psalm 74: O God, why have you rejected us forever? Why does your anger smoulder against your people? But God, you are my King from long ago, you bring salvation on the earth. Do not ignore the uproar of your enemies.

Scripture Text - John 21:15-22

The third time he said to him, "Simon son of John, do you love me?" Peter was hurt because Jesus asked him the third time, "Do you love me?" He said, "Lord, you know all things; you know that I love you." Jesus said, "Feed my sheep." John 21:17

Three times Peter denied Jesus (John 18).
Three times Jesus asks Peter, "Do you love me?"
Three times Peter says yes.
Peter was hurt. Understandably. Was this a test? A trick? A joke?
Yes – and no. Jesus was not mocking or taunting Peter, he was emphasizing the cost of loving and following Jesus. The cost of discipleship.

We don't always get things the first time. Sometimes we need a second and third try. Jesus is willing to give Peter a second chance after his three questions were affirmed. It wouldn't be easy. There would be many more challenges than two or three in Peter's life as an apostle, a follower, a disciple of his Lord Jesus.

What a privilege and a responsibility Jesus was bestowing on this follower – and on pastors today – feed my sheep.

What does it cost us today to say yes to Jesus? He calls us again to follow, to fulfill his commandments, to love and nurture brothers and sisters in Christ. Peter said yes – three times – yes.

Suggested Song: "I Have Decided To Follow Jesus"

Pray: Loving God, thank you for inviting me on this journey of faith. Help me to count the cost, and to say yes, yes, yes! In Jesus' name, Amen.

Revered Elders

In society we work against ageism, the dehumanizing of a person because they are of a certain age. Traditional cultures have honoured and revered elders. These valued members of the community were respected as repositories of wisdom, teaching, and truth-telling. Sad to say, our modern Western culture has been, since the 1960s, primarily and predominantly a youth-culture. There are hopeful signs that this is changing, and we all need to do our part to treat older adults with respect. Serving in a care home for elders, hearing their stories, listening to their hearts is a deep privilege. God never disregards us because we are older. *"Do not cast me away when I am old; do not forsake me when my strength is gone."* Psalm 71:9

Strong Through Storms, Leona

Mountain Lake, Ed

SUMMER
June - August

Be Present

We are not alone
God is with us,
No, never alone,
He promised never to leave us...
Loneliness is epidemic
seeping like a virus in big city
towers of dim light
washed by traffic shore,
or in small town basements
eating frozen dinners
wanting more.
So, the hands and feet,
the smiles and embrace
is still a human need.
Not alone but lonely
knowing another breathing warm
person may be in the apartment next
door, but they may as well
be on the next planet – may be there too.
So, be present
enflesh the care
show up, step in,
share.

Meditation – Call Out

Praying Psalm 75: I praise you, God, your name is near. I recall your wonderful work! All times and epochs are in your hand, you exalt, and you depose. As for me, I will declare this forever, I will sing praise to you, God of Jacob, for you appoint and anoint and raise up the righteous.

Scripture Text - Jonah 2:2, 7-8
In my distress I called to the LORD, and he answered me. From deep in the realm of the dead I called for help, and you listened to my cry. Jonah 2:2

The story of the renegade prophet Jonah still speaks powerfully today. Themes and images of trying to run away from God, of self-centredness, lack of faith, and discontent are perennial. When Jonah hit bottom, he prayed. I have a plaque on my desk which reads "Pray First." Sometimes I do. Often, I devise a plan, or ask for help from others before praying. Jonah heard God's call and chose to turn the other way. The overwhelming adversities flooded him with the realistic realization that propelled him to pray.

The text says, "In my distress I called to the Lord." The apostle Paul advises that we pray without ceasing. The prayer Jesus taught his disciples implies daily prayer at least – "give us this day our daily bread" – and Jonah's prayer from the deep was heard and answered.

Hopefully, we are not running from God but rather running toward God today. Jonah's problems turned to praise as he called out to God and drew a fresh breath of air.

Suggested Song: "What A Friend We Have in Jesus"

Pray: Heavenly Father, I call out to you today. Help me learn the delight and discipline of regular, submissive prayer. I thank you for hearing my prayer and for knowing my every need. I offer you grateful praise. In Jesus' name, Amen.

Is the saying, "Beauty is in the eye of the beholder" absolutely true?

Meditation – Follow the Leader

Praying Psalm 76: God, you are honoured, your name is great. You break the fiery arrows of the enemy. You are glorious and more majestic than the mountains. Human defiance only enhances your glory, for you use it as a weapon. You break the pride of Princes. Kings of the earth fear you.

Scripture Text - Joshua 1:1-2, 5-9

Have I not commanded you? Be strong and courageous. Do not be afraid; do not be discouraged, for the LORD your God will be with you wherever you go. Joshua 1:9

Succession plans can be tricky. The passing of the leadership baton to a new, perhaps a younger person sometimes is seamless and positive. Not always. In my own career there have been two apparently failed attempts at a seemingly brilliant succession plan. I say apparently, because, of course, in the end God worked both out to suit his purpose.

Moses had prepared Joshua to take the lead. Now God was acknowledging the natural fear of stepping into Moses' sandals. "Be strong" is God's admonishment. Understandably, Joshua has some fear and trepidation. We all do when stepping into new territory. God commanded him to trust (verse 5 "I will be with you"), to obey (verse 7 "Be careful to obey all the law") and get ready (verse 2 "Get ready to cross the Jordan River").

What is your "promised land" today? What new ventures or steps of obedience is God calling you to get ready for? Joshua had a role model in Moses, but our true leader is Jesus – fix your eyes on him.

Suggested Song:
"Trust and Obey"

Pray: Loving God, I thank you that you are always with me and will guide, guard, and give strength for the next steps you want me to take. I seek you for courage, boldness, and an obedient spirit. In Jesus' name, the author and perfecter of my faith, Amen.

Window Box, *Amy*

Meditation – Finishing Well

Praying Psalm 77: I cry out to you, God, listen to me! I think of you and moan, overwhelmed with longing for you. Have you rejected me forever? O God, your ways are holy. You redeemed; through Red Sea surges you made a pathway with Moses and Aaron leading the flock.

Scripture Text - Joshua 23:1-3, 6
You yourselves have seen everything the Lord your God has done to all these nations for your sake; it was the Lord your God who fought for you. Joshua 23:3

Joshua had a successful career. He was obedient, bold, hardworking, and accountable to God and to the people he served and led. "The LORD had given Israel rest from all their enemies around them" (verse 1). After years of campaigns, of conflict, and challenge, Joshua was ready to relinquish the leadership God had given him. "Joshua – a very old man" (verse 1) had served faithfully and fearlessly. When he called for his "performance evaluation" (verse 3), he was candid about God's working in his life, and all that had been collaboratively accomplished. Joshua is a model of finishing well.

When God calls us to an area of service, we are understandably aware of our weakness and limitations. Joshua relied on God's strength, grace, and empowerment throughout his life's work.

"And whatever you do, whether in word or deed, do it all in the name of the Lord Jesus, giving thanks to God the Father through him." Colossians 3:17

Suggested Song: "Take My Life and Let it Be Consecrated"

Pray: Dear God, please strengthen me to serve you faithfully. In this world that demands increasing efficiency, often with fewer resources, remind me that you call me to serve faithfully to the finish. In Jesus' name, Amen.

A Heart of Wisdom

Helen and I were visiting and sharing favourite Bible texts. We recited Psalm 23 together in the King James Version, helping each other to get through some of the parts the other had forgotten. We quoted John 3:16 and the Lord's Prayer. Then Helen said, my favourite psalm has been Psalm 90. We talked about the possibility that Moses was the author of this poem, we talked about God as our "dwelling place," our home. I shared that, as a teenager, I had set the text to music and sang the song frequently in churches and coffeehouses in the 1970s. Then she remembered and quoted, *"Teach us to number our days, that we may gain a heart of wisdom."* (Psalm 90:12) This ancient prayer was being answered right in front of me.

On the Move

God is on the move
always and forever;
We think we prefer sameness
seeing the same wallpaper, bookshelf, view;
but we really crave new.
So, God moves, in a mysterious way
wonderful, with *magnum mysterium*
while we simple beasts look on.
Look on us, O Moving Lord;
change us and make us eternally
transforming toward your likeness.
Riding on the storms of conflict,
concern, stress and struggle
Your plant your feet upon the storm
to order our norm with deep earnest
longing for reform.
As the ancient eastern saint,
Bishop of Myra, may we see storms
as evidence and opportunity:
evidence of a good God of order
stirring the waters; opportunity to
join God on the move.

Meditation – Point of View

Praying Psalm 78: O God, you speak in parables, hidden lessons from the past, stories our ancestors handed down to us. We will not hide these truths from our children. May our children, grandchildren and their grandchildren set their hopes anew on you, God – and never forget you.

Scripture Text – Jude 17-25
To the only God our Saviour be glory, majesty, power and authority, through Jesus Christ our Lord, before all ages, now and forevermore! Amen. Jude 25

Perspective changes everything. Recently, my wife and I moved to our ninth-storey condo. Our tower is situated so we get a city view as we look south, and a view of woods and mountains as we look north. Things look different from nine floors in the air. Clouds and sunsets are a fascinating, daily event. God's glory shines. Sometimes just a change of perspective can change everything.

The doxology (praise to God) in Jude is often used to conclude a worship service. In this liturgical context it sends the gathered community on their way with words of confidence, forgiveness, and freedom in Jesus Christ our Lord. Other times we can reflect on this verse in its larger context (verses 17-25) and gain fresh perspective on the challenge of living a holy, godly life in our fallen world. We re-vision our faith, prayer, and consolation in the centre of God's love (verses 20, 21).

When we set our point of view on worshipping God, we take our eyes off lesser, lower things.

Suggested Song:
"Praise God from Whom All Blessings Flow" (Doxology)

Pray: Father, I choose to lift my eyes, to worship and glorify you. Guard my mind and heart from worshipping anything else but you, now and forevermore! Amen.

Calm Water, Leona

Meditation - Lead me Lord

Praying Psalm 79: O God, pagan nations have conquered your land. O Lord, how long will you be angry with us? Help us, for the glory of your name.

Scripture Text - Judges 2: 10-16
Then the LORD raised up judges, who saved them out of the hands of these raiders. Judges 2:16

We need good leadership to enhance and enrich our lives. I am thankful for the women and men who step forward to provide leadership in our communities, in civic, provincial, and federal levels of government. Leaders in our churches, schools and businesses are key to a flourishing society. When people just do whatever seems right in their own opinion, the results can be devastating, ending in anarchy and lawlessness.

The book of Judges ends with this sad comment, *"In those days Israel had no king; everyone did as they saw fit."* (Judges 21:25)

God raises up the leaders of our times. We may question decisions and directions, but we are told to pray for and support leaders. (Romans 12) The early church found themselves in tension with the Caesars' demand to worship them and declare them lord. The Revelation of Jesus Christ at the close of the Bible gives us the necessary perspective that only Jesus is Lord: King of kings and Lord of lords. And he shall reign forever!

Suggested Song: "Saviour, Like A Shepherd Lead Us"

Pray: Loving Father, I acknowledge you as Lord and leader of my life. I pray for all in leadership, that you will grant wisdom, strength and open eyes and ears. Bless our church leaders today, in Jesus' name, Amen

In the old days, theatre stages used to have curtains. In modern theater, everything is out in the open.

Meditation – Coronation

Praying Psalm 80: Please listen, O Shepherd of Israel, O God enthroned above the cherubim, display your radiant glory. Show your mighty power. Come to rescue us! Turn us again to yourself, make your face shine down upon us. Only then will we be saved.

Scripture Text - 1 Kings 1:32-35
Then you are to go up with him, and he is to come and sit on my throne and reign in my place. I have appointed him ruler over Israel and Judah. 1 Kings 1:35

King David needed to take quick action. The kingdom was in danger of imploding, dissolving into civil war. Eventually this happened anyway a few years later, but for now, the Davidic rule was established. Prophets, priests, temple officials were called to enact the coronation of the new king, Solomon. Kings come and go. Federal governments come and go. Nations come and go. We await the one who has come and will come again, King Jesus. And he shall reign forever and ever. *"On his robe and on his thigh, he has this name written: KING OF KINGS AND LORD OF LORDS."* Revelation 19:16.

The terms "kingdom" and "lord" may seem antiquated, but the concept is current. Who is sovereign in your life? Who do you worship? Who is King? Who is Lord?

Suggested Song: "All Hail King Jesus"

Pray: Heavenly Father, you sent your son into the world to draw us into your eternal kingdom. Your kingdom come, your will be done – in my life, and in our world today. In the name of King Jesus, Amen.

It Always Lifts My Spirits

One of the things that makes life at Tabor Village vibrant and alive is having visiting choirs and special music groups from the community. Often made up of seniors from local churches, or sometimes children from local schools, these groups provide uplifting music, smiling faces and a sense of energy, and the awareness that the residents are not forgotten. It is an expression of love that communicates "You matter." Residents come into the Living Room, expectant, sometimes having been told a music group was coming. Molly would frequently express her joy at the news that a music group was visiting. "It always lifts my spirits," she would say.

Zenith of Light

I want to walk as a child of the light
I want to be like Jesus. (Gospel song)

Nicodemus came at night
confused and confusing
sarcastic, sardonic
questioning, questing
the well-wishing Samaritan woman
met Jesus at the blaze of noon
the zenith of Light
      listened, learned, compelled, concerned
      shared, cared – was spared.
Judas went out of the Upper Room – it was night
Jesus prayed the garden prayer and was betrayed
at night
But seaside barbeque and Emmaus interview
were daylight talks and walks.
dawn and dusk
questions and trust
thrust out of darkness into
Resurrection Light!

Meditation – A Person of Prayer

Praying Psalm 81: I sing to you, God, my strength. I hear your voice say, "Now I will take the weight from your shoulders." I choose to follow you, walk in your paths, receive your blessings of finest wheat and wild honey from the rock.

Scripture Text - 1 Kings 17:1, James 5:17-19
Now Elijah the Tishbite, from Tishbe in Gilead, said to Ahab, "As the LORD, the God of Israel, lives, whom I serve, there will be neither dew nor rain in the next few years except at my word. 1 Kings 17:1

Elijah was a man who lived in Israel in the ninth century BC. He needed to eat and drink, rest and work, just like any other person. He was also called to a particular prophetic task during the reign of King Ahab in Jerusalem. Elijah was a troublemaker, according to Ahab and his wife Jezebel. But he was very kind to a widow in the village of Zarephath (1 Kings 1:7-24). He exhibited prophetic boldness (1 Kings 18:16-39) and he was a person of prayer (verses 42-46). He also experienced severe doubt and depression (1 Kings 19:3-18).

God used Elijah in powerful and dramatic ways. Elijah also experienced the challenges of everyday life and had his annoying issues to deal with. Through all these realities, he was a person of prayer (James 5:17-19). Prayer moves the hand of God. Prayer changes the course of history. Prayer is our most important task.

Let us live as believers who pray.

Suggested Song: "Lord, Listen to Your Children Praying"

Pray: Thank you, dear Lord, for the wonderful privilege of prayer. I embrace the power and importance of being a person of prayer. As I praise, confess, intercede, and thank you in regular prayer, please work in our world. In Jesus' name, Amen.

Mountaintop meetings open our eyes to surprise.

Valley vitality strengthens heart and hand.

Meditation – How Can I Help You?

Praying Psalm 82: God, you preside as the heavenly judge; give justice to the poor, the orphan, the oppressed, and the destitute. We are mere mortals; rise up, O God, and judge the earth.

Scripture Text - 2 Kings 4:1-7
Elisha replied to her, "How can I help you? Tell me, what do you have in your house?"
"Your servant has nothing there at all," she said, "except a small jar of olive oil."
2 Kings 4:2

We sometimes need to ask the simple questions in life, like "How can I help you?" The demands of life are often overwhelming. Family pressures, financial problems, social justice issues, climate change and natural disasters – the problems are complex and seemingly out of control.

The story from 2 Kings 4 is encouraging. It is practical. It asks an important foundational question and proceeds to provide a practical solution.

After Elisha asks the destitute woman the opening question, he follows it with a problem-solving methodology: "What do you have in your house?" Beginning with what we have in hand, what God has provided us, we then open ourselves to ways in which God wants to bless us.

Sometimes in our philanthropic zeal, we overlook this important step. How can the person with the need bring what they have, to help solve the problem? In the widow's case, she had only a small jar of olive oil, but she also had supportive neighbours. She reached out and the result was blessing. Whom have you asked recently, "How can I help you?"

Suggested Song: "Make Me a Blessing"

Pray: Loving and providing God, you know the people in my life who are in need. Help me have the love and courage to ask how I can help. Then, Lord, please provide the answer and resources so we can collaborate to meet the need. For your glory and for the benefit of others, in Jesus' name, Amen.

Hand Down, Ray

Meditation – Show a Little Kindness

Praying Psalm 83: O God do not be silent! Do not be deaf. Do not be quiet, O God. Don't you see and hear the corruption? The nations are yours, the leaders, the people need to learn that you alone are called the Lord, that you alone are the most high, supreme over all the earth.

Scripture Text - 2 Kings 25:27-30
He spoke kindly to him and gave him a seat of honour higher than those of the other kings who were with him in Babylon. 2 Kings 25:28

Most people are immigrating to this country from all over the world. Our nation has been home to Indigenous peoples who have lived and thrived on this continent for millenia. Most of our families have emigrated from somewhere else on the planet. To some extent, literally or figuratively, we are all newcomers and exiles. Jehoiachin, the deposed king of Judah, was in exile. His was a forced emigration. He experienced hardship, loss, and deprivation. Then he was shown a little kindness. The Babylonian king Awel-Marduk gave Jehoiachin a place of honour and provided for all his needs. We don't know exactly what motivated this act of kindness but it was certainly exceptional.

There are people in our lives today who need an act of kindness shown to them. It may be simply a kind word, or a gesture of encouragement. It may involve something more from us. As followers of Jesus, we have more than enough motivation to serve others in the name of our Servant-King Jesus.

Suggested Song: "The Love of God"

Pray: Heavenly Father, help me be a person of kindness, gentleness, and goodness – may the fruit of the Holy Spirit be growing and evident in my life today – for your glory, in Jesus' name, Amen.

Strength For Today And Bright Hope For Tomorrow

At the close of daily prayer time, I would make my rounds to greet each person who had attended. Frequently, I would receive words of encouragement and thanks from residents. Audrey would always say, "Thank you. That gives me strength for today and bright hope for tomorrow." She knew she was quoting from the refrain of "Great Is Thy Faithfulness." Something had connected with her spirit, and she needed to tell me. I waited for it, and she never disappointed. Was it a mechanical response? Was it habit? No, it was genuine, heartfelt and a personal spiritual practice which served as part of the liturgy. Audrey perpetuated the work of the people, and through it, the Holy Spirit spoke to my heart.

Olivet Discourse

All of it on Olivet
needed to be said:
admiration for a beautiful
stone vault, flying buttress
or keystone in the arch
are all fine in their place...
but all will crumble
watch, wait, anticipate
walls are built slowly
but can collapse in moments
not one left upon another.

Some days the wait
seems intolerable
some days the weight
seems intolerable.
Keep watch – don't be misled
by false Messiahs'
rabbit trails, eschatological
derails
Olivet riveted their eyes
on Jesus, kept them from bolting
– although in a few days
they would flee
for this hour
this discourse set their future.

Meditation – Great is Thy Faithfulness

Praying Psalm 84: How lovely is your dwelling place, O Lord of heaven's armies. I long, yes, I faint with longing to enter the courts of the Lord. What joy for those whose strength comes from the Lord, who have set their minds on a pilgrimage to Jerusalem. A single day in your courts is better than a thousand elsewhere. I would rather be a gatekeeper in the house of the Lord than live in the homes of the wicked.

Scripture Text - Lamentations 3:19-26
Because of the LORD's great love we are not consumed, for his compassions never fail. They are new every morning; great is your faithfulness. Lamentations 3:22-23

We seldom use the word "lament" in modern conversation except perhaps lightheartedly, as in "They are lamenting the loss of their favourite ice cream flavour." To seriously lament is to mourn out loud, to visibly express sorrow, to wail and weep for a tremendous loss. The prophet Jeremiah was sometimes referred to as the weeping prophet because of his laments recorded in the appropriately entitled book, *Lamentations*.

In this carefully structured expression of intense grief over the demise of Jerusalem, the author brings order to dismay, structure to hopelessness. Four of the five chapters (1,2,4,5) each have twenty-two verses, each verse beginning with a letter of the Hebrew alphabet in sequence. Chapter three – the middle chapter of this short book – has sixty-six letters (three times twenty-two) symbolizing intensity and excessive grief. Right in the centre of this longer chapter (3:19-26), using the literary structure known as a chiasm, is this exquisite expression of hope and confidence. A shining gem of faith in the centre of chaos. "Great is thy faithfulness."

God is faithful to meet us in the middle of our worst situations to provide compassion and mercy.

Suggested Song: "Great Is Thy Faithfulness"

Pray: Our faithful, loving God, thank you for meeting me in the painful times of life. Thank you for your awareness and care for our nations and for this fallen world. In your loving faithfulness I trust today. In Jesus' name, Amen.

Learning a name is educational.
Earning a name is reputational.
Naming a child is aspirational.
Naming a town after yourself is egotistical.
Knowing God's name is inspirational.
Hearing God call your name – transformational.

Meditation – Glory!

Praying Psalm 85: Lord, you poured out blessings on your land! Restore us again, O God of our salvation. Surely your salvation is near to those who fear you. Love and Truth have met, Righteousness and Peace have kissed. May Righteousness herald your steps.

Scripture Text – Leviticus 9:23-24
Moses and Aaron then went into the tent of meeting. When they came out, they blessed the people; and the glory of the LORD appeared to all the people. Leviticus 9:23

When I see an amazing sunrise or sunset, or freshly fallen snow on distant mountains, or see a cascading waterfall, it evokes a sense of awe, majesty, and great delight. At an immeasurably higher level is the majesty and awe of Yahweh's glory. We can only catch a glimpse of God's glory. The LORD allowed the gathered worshippers at the tent of meeting to receive the blessing of Moses and Aaron, which preceded God choosing to reveal something of his great glory. In the person of Jesus Christ, God in the flesh, we see glory, grace, and truth. The apostle John records in John 1:14, *"The Word became flesh and made his dwelling among us. We have seen his glory, the glory of the one and only Son, who came from the Father, full of grace and truth."*

When we wish someone God's blessing, we are expressing a sincere desire that they will experience fullness, wellbeing, that they will flourish and be well. When the people received the blessing of their special leaders and witnessed a dramatic outpouring of divine presence, they shouted for joy and fell facedown (verse 24).

Suggested Song "To God Be the Glory"

Pray: Great God, I give you praise and honour for your awesome glory and immeasurable blessings. In humble gratitude I give you thanks, in Jesus' name, Amen.

Meditation – Celebration

Praying Psalm 86: Hear my prayer, Lord, and answer me, for I am poor and needy. Guard my life for I am faithful to you. Bring joy to your servant, Lord, for I put my trust in you.

Scripture Text - Leviticus 23:1-2, 44

The LORD said to Moses, "Speak to the Israelites and say to them: 'These are my appointed festivals, the appointed festivals of the LORD, which you are to proclaim as sacred assemblies.'"
Leviticus 23:1-2

Everyone enjoys a good celebration. Every culture has appointed days to have a party, give and receive gifts, enjoy good food and drink, and celebrate the goodness of life and relationships. Whether a birthday, anniversary, Christmas, graduation – or a religious "holy-day" – we look forward to celebrations. Being in relationship with the living God is reason to rejoice. In Leviticus 23, Moses was instructed to inaugurate seven holy festivals and observances: the weekly Sabbath (verse 3), the seven-day long Passover and the Festival of Unleavened Bread observances (verses 4-8), Offering the Firstfruits (verses 9-14), the Festival of Weeks (verses 15-22), the Festival of Trumpets (verses 23-25), the Day of Atonement (verses 26-32), the Festival of Tabernacles (verses 33-36).

The Creator God is beyond time and space, but because they are God's good gifts to people, both time and space are honoured in specific and meaningful ways. We may not observe some of these traditional celebrations (we all are called to remember and observe sabbath every week), but we do well to honour God's creation of special times and specific places in our personal and corporate lives. *"This is the day which the LORD hath made; we will rejoice and be glad in it."* Psalm 118:24

Suggested Song: "This Is the Day"

Pray: Almighty God, you are beyond the limitations of time and space, yet you meet us in meaningful ways in our daily lives and at special festive occasions. We celebrate in your goodness, in Jesus' name, Amen.

It Was Her Gift

Annie was always so deeply thankful to Jesus for everything. Annie would say, "I don't know how people get through life without Jesus." Her simple and profound conversational prayer was uplifting. Bedridden with very limited mobility, her beautiful smile and spirit of love and grace emanated from her room. She would pray for friends and lift them into God's presence. I am thankful she shared it so freely.

Remembrance, Ray

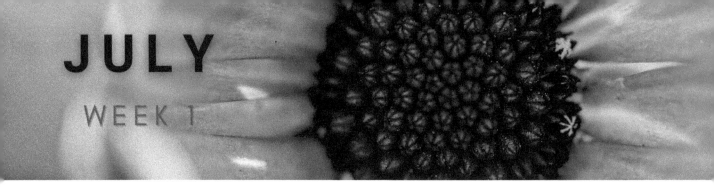

JULY
WEEK 1

Praying Psalm 87: O Lord, you have established holy places on this earth. All people and all lands will acknowledge you. Babylon, Philistia, Tyre, Iran, Kenya, Russia, Peru... We praise you with songs springing from God-made fountains.

In Your Presence

Of all the paths there are to walk
I choose to follow you, Lord.
Of all the roads that lie ahead,
Your way will be for me.
So many doors, so many rooms
Appealing to our senses.
But where they lead and what they hold
May keep us from your presence.
The voices call, the crowd attracts,
It's hard to stay on track, Lord.
From all around we hear the sounds
That keep us from Your presence.
I take a stand, I make a choice,
I'm walking in your strength,
The armour's on,
The prayers begun,
Lord, keep me in your presence.

Meditation – The Blessing of An Elder

Praying Psalm 88: Lord, you are the God who saved me. Day and night I cry out to you. I am overwhelmed with troubles, and I am close to death. I'm in the dark, I feel your wrath. All my friends are gone, it is dark.

Scripture Text - Luke 2:25-35
Then Simeon blessed them and said to Mary, his mother: "This child is destined to cause the falling and rising of many in Israel, and to be a sign that will be spoken against, so that the thoughts of many hearts will be revealed. And a sword will pierce your own soul too."
Luke 2:34-35

I still can see him lifting our six-month-old son in the spotlight, with his eyes raised to the sky, reciting these words, "... my eyes have seen your salvation..." It was our church Christmas program, and this elder pastor agreed to play the role of Simeon, and our son served as baby Jesus. Though the lines were spoken in a pageant, they were filled with sincerity and life experience. This octogenarian was a godly man who truly blessed us all that day.

When an elder Christian blesses another person, there is a sense of the presence and pleasure of God. The church has always taken blessings and benedictions (good words) seriously. The Bible is full of blessings, including this text often quoted or spoken during Christmas. Simeon blessing points ahead to Calvary and deep soul-piercing. And it also sings of light, salvation, fulfilment.

This text is one of the Christmas songs, referred to as the *Nunc Dimittis*, (now dismiss). Give and receive a blessing today.

Suggested Song: "Make Me A Blessing"

Pray: Father, thank you for the many blessings we receive from your hand. Help me see an opportunity today to extend a blessing to someone, whether in word or action. In Jesus' name, Amen.

A restless heart is a good thing only as it wrestles our soul into the very presence of God.

Meditation – Stirring Words

Praying Psalm 89: I will sing of your great love forever; with my mouth I will make known your faithfulness to all generations. The heavens also praise you; you are Lord of all. Tabor and Hermon sing for joy. I am blessed as I walk in the light of your presence.

Scripture Text – Luke 4:18-21
The Spirit of the Lord is on me, because he has anointed me to proclaim good news to the poor.
He has sent me to proclaim freedom for the prisoners and recovery of sight for the blind,
to set the oppressed free, to proclaim the year of the Lord's favour. Luke 4:18-19

The Holy Spirit anointed and appointed Jesus to read that particular text from Isaiah on that particular day, in that particular synagogue, in that particular way. His home church. Neighbours who saw him grow up would have been there. Two startling things about that sabbath day's reading of Isaiah 61 - The first was that Jesus stopped at the words "to proclaim the year of the Lord's favour" (verse 19) because the full text goes on to say, "and the day of vengeance of our God." It was no careless omission – Jesus intended to leave the listeners lingering on the words of the Lord's favour. But the bigger shock was his eight-word application, "Today this scripture is fulfilled in your hearing." A transformative if brief sermon. It stirred some to speak well of Jesus (verse 22) and others to be furious (verse 28). Jesus' words and works still have that effect.

Suggested Song: "There Is a Redeemer"

Pray: Lord, help me to truly hear your word of truth and power today, and choose to follow you more intentionally than ever, in Jesus' name I pray, Amen.

Tozer and Team by Ray Harris

Meditation – Lost and Found

Praying Psalm 90: Lord, you have been our dwelling place through all our generations. Even before the world was formed, you are the everlasting God. Life is so short, we're like the morning grass that grows and is cut down at night. Teach me to make each day count. Establish and bless my work.

Scripture Text – Luke 15:1-7
Now the tax collectors and sinners were all gathering around to hear Jesus. But the Pharisees and the teachers of the law muttered, "This man welcomes sinners and eats with them." Luke 15:1-2

We have all experienced the frustration and sometimes even panic of losing something valuable. From elementary school lost & found bins to the resident in a care home trying to locate a lost item, we search diligently until we find the lost possession. How much greater is the intensity and deep divine desire for Jesus to find the lost. He was accused by the establishment of spending time with the wrong people. But they were exactly the people who were lost and needed to be found. So, in classic Jesus-style he tells a story. In fact, he tells three stories in Luke 15 to really make the point. The stories are familiar: the lost sheep, the lost coin, the lost son. They all describe the state of lostness, then tell of the search using words like "go after" (verse 4), "search carefully" (verse 8), "was filled with compassion" (verse 20). And the result in each recovery was joy, celebration, restoration. Oh, the deep, deep love of Jesus.

Suggested Song: "Amazing Grace"

Pray: Thank you, loving Father, for your divine search party. I once was lost, but now I am found, thank you, Jesus. In your name I pray, Amen.

Travel Through Memories Recalled

I love the province of BC. Growing up in Vancouver, I had often travelled up Howe Sound, over to Vancouver Island, and up the Sunshine Coast. In later years I travelled more extensively throughout the province, coming to appreciate the Slocan Valley, the Okanagan, Kootenays, and Columbia Valley regions. I enjoyed many conversations about places in BC where residents and tenants had lived and worked. Often one memory would unlock a door to a flood of stories. Pauline could tell many interesting stories about growing up in the Slocan Valley. Her father ran the general store, and she got to know many people as they came for supplies. Her eyes glistened as she recalled childhood memories.

Poems for Suburbia

I.   Vinyl-clad in rows they stand
Sentinels on reformed land,
Cloning, cloistered, claustrophobic
Living spaces - built to plan.
All for comfort, all for ease,
Instant lawns and instant trees
Perfect plants in perfect borders
Landscaped traces - on demand.
Insulated spaces grow
Where meadow-bloom and water flow
Sated systems, infrastructure
Inter-link yet isolate.   October 1994

II.   Suburbia's grandeur out shaken!
No spirit but the developers, hover over head for
Cover for quick release for quicker sale.
Location lowers the occasion of beauty
As double-doors, double-driveways
Double the dweller's determination to discover
Life in vehicle village...
Life in the no-lane, as all is upfront!   March 1995

III.   Fairfield, Country Meadows, Cedar Ridge, all names designed
to shape the mind to outdoor places and natural spaces.
Street names themed with common roots; Oak and Birch and Holly
Street, or names of towns of simpler times.
Neighbors made by moving in - moving up, moving on.
Do more than names and floorplans draw people together? Community
as unity grows from togetherness. Sharing property lines, family times,
outdoor tasks, Halloween masks -and treats! Despite seeming artificial,
superficial, community can grow in subdivisions.
We've seen it, and know it is so.   March 1995

Meditation – What's *Minas* is Yours

☀ **Praying Psalm 91:** Lord, I seek you, to dwell in your shelter, O most high. To rest in your Almighty shadow. You are my refuge and fortress; in you I trust. You will save me from snares, traps, attacks, and give me confidence and courage. You command your angels to guard me in all my ways. I call on you and you answer.

📖 **Scripture Text** – Luke 19:1-26
"Well done, my good servant!" his master replied. "Because you have been trustworthy in a very small matter, take charge of ten cities." Luke 19:17

Each of us has been given gifts, abilities, strengths, talents. We sometimes develop them in childhood or youth, and sometimes later in life. These gifts are on loan to us to use or refuse. They are given to us by our Heavenly Father for the benefit of others, to the glory of God, and for our enrichment and growth. One of the astounding things about God's resources is that he asks us to manage them, to be stewards. We can be good stewards, or we can squander what has been entrusted. One foundational gift we have all received in our temporal world is the gift of time. While we are breathing, we all have twenty-four hours each day. Some are given longer or shorter lives, but it is all a gift to be appreciated and wisely shared.

In this parable of Luke 19, three servants were each given ten *minas* (verse 13) or about three months' wages. When the accounting was done, the master gave the various rewards in proportion to their trustworthiness. All that we have is God's. God loans us life, breath, time, money, ability, and we are to be good and faithful servants. What's ours is his.

🎵 **Suggested Song:** "Count Your Blessings"

🙏 **Pray:** Father in heaven, you are the giver of every good and perfect gift. Thank you. Grant wisdom, discipline, and a faithful heart as I invest your gifts in your kingdom, for your glory and others' blessing, in Jesus' name, Amen.

To pull back the curtain for a peek is not nearly the same as allowing God to remove the veil.

Meditation – Opened Minds

Praying Psalm 92: It is so good to praise you, Lord, to make music to your name, O most high. To proclaim your love in the morning and your faithfulness at night. Lord, let me flourish like a palm tree or like a cedar planted and growing in your presence. I want to still bear fruit in old age, help me stay fresh and green.

Scripture Text – Luke 24:44-53
Then he opened their minds so they could understand the Scriptures. Luke 24:45

A favourite hymn of mine makes the request "May the mind of Christ my Savior dwell in me from day to day." A favorite author of mine talks about growing up inside a mind so large that there is no sense of claustrophobia. While I'm sharing favourites, Luke's account of Jesus' appearing to his disciples is heart-warming. A favourite.

We need to have our minds opened by Jesus, regularly We need the Holy Spirit as our Teacher as we read, study, meditate and live the scriptures. Jesus' birth, life, ministry, passion, death, resurrection, and ascension all need to be rehearsed and celebrated. This is why the church calendar observes these seasons throughout the year, every year, so we remember the story of Jesus. As Jesus taught his disciples to read the entire Bible in light of him. when we do, our minds are opened.

Suggested Song: "May the Mind of Christ my Saviour"

Pray: Lord God, may the mind of Christ my Saviour live in me from day to day, by his love and power controlling all I do and say. Amen.

Flowing Stream, Leona

Meditation – Prepare the Way

Praying Psalm 93: Lord, you reign! Robed in majesty, armed with strength, the world is established firm and secure because you are from eternity. Your statutes are firm, holiness adorns you for endless days.

Scripture Text – Malachi 2:17-3:5

"I will send my messenger, who will prepare the way before me. Then suddenly the Lord you are seeking will come to his temple; the messenger of the covenant, whom you desire, will come," says the LORD Almighty. Malachi 3:1

John the Baptist was sent to prepare the way for Jesus, the long-awaited Messiah. John's message was a stern one of repentance and changed behaviours. Tax collectors were to stop their corrupt schemes, soldiers were to act justly, and those who repented of their sins and were baptized by John were told to share their possessions with the poor. This was a radical renunciation of their sinful past.

In these ways and others, John the Baptizer was preparing for the harvest that Jesus would usher in. Mark's gospel quotes Malachi 3:1 as well as Isaiah 40 as context for the message and ministry of John.

In gardening and farming, before the seeds are sown, the soil must be prepared. Cultivating, clearing out the weeds, allowing oxygen into the soil, adding manure and humus so the soil can release nutrients to the maturing plant. What do I need to do today to prepare the way for Jesus to have a fruitful, abundant harvest in my life?

Suggested Song: "We Plough the Fields and Scatter"

Pray: Lord Jesus, I repent of my sin today. I turn back to you with the desire that you will help me be kind and generous with people in my life. Help me to see needs around me, and to allow you to do your good gardening in my life. In Jesus' name, Amen.

The Garden

The courtyard at Tabor Home has several raised garden beds for residents to plant their own gardens. On a nice May day after Victoria Day weekend, I enjoyed helping folks plant their annuals. Ernie chose to plant by colour schemes; Wilma knew the names of the specific plants she wanted, marigolds, petunias, Shasta daisy, rudbeckia, alyssum. Planting gardens together provides good opportunities to chat. We would talk about gardens they used to have in their yards and on their balconies. The warmth of the sunshine brought out the aromas of the plants. We could hear birdsong when conversation lulled. It was a very nice way to connect with people and enjoy the sounds, smells, and textures of the garden.

No Swaying Reed

no swaying reed, no finely dressed preacher,
but a rugged wilderness man
rough attire, unrefined tastes:
beard dripped with honey,
locust breath.
Jesus watched the crowds
maybe smiled at his up-country cousin
confronting vipers reared for regard.
Throngs longed for renewal,
repented relented
went under Jordan flow to know
 they had been in the hands
 of someone wiser than they: the Baptizer.
When he recoiled at Yeshua's request
 to join the current trend
his gentle words made sweet by honey,
"I should be baptized by you."
Reassured that heaven heard
rising up from muddy tide
Greeted by Dove blessing,
Father's voice caressing
The Three took the day in stride.

Meditation – Quiet Place

Praying Psalm 94: You are an avenging God, rise up and judge the earth. You know the futility of human plants; discipline us, teach us, grant relief. Your consolation changes anxiety to joy!

Scripture Text – Mark 1:29-39
Very early in the morning, while it was still dark, Jesus got up, left the house and went off to a solitary place, where he prayed. Mark 1:35

Working in the Kingdom of God can be exhausting. Jesus, fully God, also fully man, needed solitude. He had healed all who were brought to him. Even in the small circle of friends, he was constantly available to minister, and healed Simon's mother-in-law (verse 31). Jesus knew he needed solitude to refocus and prepare for further ministry (verses 36-39). Solitude is one of the Christian disciplines. We are sometimes uncomfortable with silence and solitude. Prayer is the restoration of relationship with our Heavenly Father. Jesus modelled it regularly. We are to be people of prayer, as Jesus was, and that takes intentional time alone with God. Often it requires getting away from others, maybe early in the morning,

The dual themes in Jesus' life of prayer and service are to be the energizing reality of our spiritual lives as well. Prayer changes us and it changes the world. In prayer we bring the unseen realities before the all-seeing God and gain fresh perspective, hope, and joy for another day of grace.

Suggested Song:
"There Is a Quiet Place"

Pray: Father, I take this time to become still, to acknowledge your presence, peace and power in this space of solitude. Thank you for giving me strength. In Jesus' name, Amen.

God's grace shines and shouts in my weakness.

Meditation – Go Home

Praying Psalm 95: Today, if I hear your voice, let me receive it with a soft, open heart. I praise you and invite others to join. Forgive us when we go astray, allow us to enter your rest.

Scripture Text – Mark 5:18-20
Jesus did not let him, but said, "Go home to your own people and tell them how much the Lord has done for you, and how he has had mercy on you." Mark 5:19

Do you ever question where God has placed you? Maybe in your workplace, or the church you attend, or areas of service in the community? It is a common reality as humans to question and sometimes feel discontent. Our text seems to indicate that this miraculously, dramatically healed man really wanted to go with Jesus. Think of the powerful testimony this formerly demon-possessed outcast would have. His story would draw crowds.

Instead, Jesus sent him home to minister to his own people, telling them about God's mercy. Did this man question the assignment? We don't know, but we read that he shared his story with his neighbours, and they were amazed.

As we faithfully, quietly, sincerely serve where God places us, we leave the results to God. We can only see such a very small part of the much larger reality. Where has God called you to serve today? In your home, your neighbourhood, your workplace, your church. Little is much when God is in it.

Suggested Song: "Little Is Much When God Is in It"

Pray: Thank you, Lord, for the place you have me serving you today. I am the only one who can reach these people in the unique way you have gifted me. Forgive me for feelings of discontent, doubt, and discouragement. Use me today, Lord, for your glory and the blessing of those in my life, in Jesus' name, Amen.

Among the Grass, Amy

Meditation – No Offence

Praying Psalm 96: A new song I sing to you, join me, earth. I declare your glory, marvellous works, greatness, honour, and majesty. Come worship God with me, family, community, nations. Even trees and seas sing for joy before the Lord, for he is coming.

Scripture Text - Mark 6:1-6
"Isn't this the carpenter? Isn't this Mary's son and the brother of James, Joseph, Judas and Simon? Aren't his sisters here with us?" And they took offence at him. Mark 6:3

People take offence at things very easily. Sometimes the way we dress or talk or eat or walk can set someone off. I have my pet peeves. Little, inconsequential things that have no real significance. Usually, it is when a machine or piece of technology malfunctions! I frequently confess this small-mindedness.

The people in Jesus' town took offence at almost everything about him. His occupation, his parentage, his family background. Today, people can take offence at the followers of Jesus for many reasons. Some of the reasons are valid: hypocrisy, lack of compassion and love for others, being preachy or judgmental. But sometimes people take offence for very petty reasons.

When Jesus' hometown friends took offence at him, the consequences were significant. Their affront, skepticism, and critical attitudes blocked them from receiving what Jesus could give them.

We all are guilty at times of taking offence at something or someone. What blessings are we blocking when we let our feelings of pride and judgmentalism blind us to a blessing?

Suggested Song: "I Surrender All"

Pray: Father, forgive me for being easily offended. I know that it is pride that causes me to move to a posture of criticism and judgmentalism. Help me see where you want to bless me today. I am open to your grace. In Jesus' name, Amen.

Pray First

As chaplain at Tabor, I had a plaque on my office desk reading "Pray First." I wish I could say that I always followed the advice, but I did make a concerted effort to pray weekly with staff. Monday mornings a few of us would meet for prayer. We committed the day and the week ahead to God. We prayed for residents and families, we prayed for leadership, for our supporting churches, for the city of Abbotsford. Ronda instigated it. She was a faithful pray-er. We prayed standing in the front office, so anyone who was passing through could take a moment and join. Monday morning prayer symbolized the desire and objective to "Pray First."

JULY
WEEK 4

Garden Time

always mildly disappointing
   those tiny fragments of color
   tentative transplants
   painstakingly pried apart and planted in rows or in clusters
following the foliage of fading tulips and daffodils
   the bare, clean soil seems barren boring bereft
   except for the almost embarrassing newcomers
        bedding plants
   (marigold alyssum petunia)
always mildly disappointing, almost pitiful how small and
   inconsequential those seedlings were

sensing my disillusionment dad would dig
   "good things come in small packages"
   returning his smile to indicate I got it
        – almost –
over summer time the annuals
   grew spread filled the open
       space exceeding expectation

always mildly disappointing
   those other times – sometimes
   falling short of annual expectations
   ....give them garden time...

Meditation - Listen to Him!

Praying Psalm 97: Lord, you are King! You are surrounded by clouds and thick darkness; inscrutable righteousness and justice are your foundation. May I never worship anything less than you. Light dawns for me, joy and rejoicing in you, I give thanks.

Scripture Text - Mark 9:2-8
Then a cloud appeared and covered them, and a voice came from the cloud: "This is my Son, whom I love. Listen to him!" Mark 9:7

The account of the Transfiguration of Jesus should be celebrated each year. In the church calendar it usually falls in February during the season of Epiphany. We observe Christmas, Easter and Holy Week and we should also remember Pentecost, Ascension and the Transfiguration. The disciples were invited up the mountain – which is not named in the gospels, but tradition suggests that it was Mount Tabor. They witnessed the amazing transfiguration of Jesus in radiant clothing and a glory-illuminated face. They saw Moses and Elijah talking with Jesus about his upcoming exodus – his passion, death, and resurrection. The climax was to hear a Voice saying, "This is my Son, whom I love. Listen to him!"
John later testified to this event (1 John 1).

Listen to him! All authority is given to Jesus. We go in that authority and share with others how Jesus has changed our lives. That is what Peter, James and John did – and the world has never been the same.

Suggested Song: "Freely, Freely You Have Received"

Pray: Loving Father, thank you for sending your Son. Holy Spirit, give us joy and courage in sharing the Jesus story. In his name, Amen.

Masterpieces stand the test of time. We are God's masterpiece.

Meditation – Childlike

Praying Psalm 98: I will keep singing a new song for all your marvellous works and victory. You remember your steadfast love and faithfulness. My praise mingles with other earthlings: musicians, oceans, continents, hills, rivers... for you will judge the world with righteousness and all people with equity.

Scripture Text – Mark 10:13-16
Truly I tell you, anyone who will not receive the kingdom of God like a little child will never enter it. Mark 10:15

Having children around you changes your life. Whether they are your children or grandchildren, nephews or nieces, or children from your community, children bring energy, life, and laughter. And usually some noise!

I'm glad the old cranky adage, "Children should be seen and not heard," has in most circles been replaced by, "Let the children come."

What is it about a childlike approach that Jesus affirmed when he said, receive me ... like a little child? It is not childish outbursts like temper tantrums, bossing other kids around, or misbehaving (let's be honest, children aren't angels). Rather, Jesus was affirming the attributes of love, trust, simplicity, joy and curiosity that children exude. Children are also persistent – we need persistence in our prayer and worship life. Children are always learning – we need to be lifelong learners. And children can make us laugh.

Everyone enjoys a good laugh. Apparently, even Jesus.

Suggested Song: "Jesus Loves Me"

Pray: Dear God, I come to you like a trusting child today. Thank you that you are my Heavenly Father, and you welcome me, just like you welcomed and blessed the children. I depend on you, Father, and I pray in Jesus' name, Amen.

Fisher, Hudson

144

Meditation – O Mortal

Praying Psalm 99: Your sovereign presence demands reverence, fear, obedience. I must tremble. You are holy, mighty, lover of justice and righteousness. I keep learning from Moses, Aaron, and Samuel, among many others who called on your name.

Scripture Text – Micah 6:6-8
He has shown you, O mortal, what is good. And what does the LORD require of you? To act justly and to love mercy and to walk humbly with your God. Micah 6:8

Our world is filled with so much injustice. Racism, poverty, addiction, world hunger and homelessness. How can we as human beings treat each other so horribly? A one-word answer: sin. Sin makes humans take what isn't theirs, lie to each other and to themselves, be greedy, proud, lustful, hateful. Rebellion against God in all its forms results in devastating injustice. Even when people try to live a good life. Even if we sacrifice and put on a good show, try to convince others of our piety (Micah 6:6,7), God waves it all away and says – act justly, love mercy, humble yourself.

We are mortal. God is God – we are not. We are called to walk humbly with God by loving the things God loves (mercy for the oppressed) and living life with care and concern for other mortals (justice). To take the hand of Jesus. To lean on his strength. To learn from his justice, mercy, and grace.

Suggested Song: "Unity"

Pray: Forgive us, Lord, for we have sinned. Forgive us for individual and national acts of injustice. Help us live in the renewing, rebirthing power of Jesus as your children, empowered by your Holy Spirit, we humbly pray in Jesus' name, Amen.

A Special Request

Residents come to Tabor Home and Valhaven to live until they die. Death is uncomfortable to talk about, and certainly experiencing the death of a loved one is painful. In 2018, Tabor incorporated the practice of an Honour Guard to honour the life and memory of one who has died. A beautiful, handmade butterfly quilt is placed over the body, and we accompany the funeral director as the gurney makes its way to the front door. In the several processions I led, I would play a favourite song on my device as we walked down the hall. Usually, the song was a familiar hymn, but Rose had made a special request: "Rum and Coca-Cola," sung by the Andrews Sisters. The family and staff smiled and gently swayed to the rhythm. Rose would have loved it.

Sonnets By Seashore

1.

Jesus appeared, but no one could know where;
on road, through walls, or on a seashore calm.
Waves now stilled, a new impediment from
lack of fish, lack of luck – and too much care.
Until that early morning call out there
His seashore voice rings out like prayer, like psalm,
"Friends," He called them who hid when death had come,
"Have you no fish?" No luck, but grief to share.
They listened to this Voice, and then they cast;
their bursting net they lugged, with joy perspire,
dragging obedient catch collapse at last
at His feet, showing scars of His desire.
But not before the Rock, stripped down, swam fast
to meet their Seashore Lord and gaze on fire.

(John 21:1-9)

2.

They broke their fast complete with fish and bread.
In silence chewed, digested disbelief.
Recalling hillside meals which brought relief,
None dared ask their questions – they knew, they fed.
Yet questions lapped at seashore minds, and said
How could He live? How eat and share their grief?
They saw Him hang and thirst and die like thief?
They saw His spear-pierced side and left Him dead.
Their questions ebbed, subsumed by three great waves
as Jesus asked the Rock, "Do you love me?"
Well-fed, the fishers see how he behaves
and how responds to burning questions. Three
times asked, sad echoes of how he betrays.
Now giv'n the joy, the task to feed by sea.

146

Meditation – How Tempting

Praying Psalm 100: I join with countless others to make a joyful noise to worship with gladness to enter your presence with singing. I know you are God. You made me, you guide me, you provide all I need. May my children, grandchildren, and all generations acknowledge your steadfast, enduring love.

Scripture Text - Matthew 4:1-11
The tempter came to him and said, "If you are the Son of God, tell these stones to become bread." Matthew 4:3

Temptation always begins with an "if." The planting of the seed of doubt, of questioning, of prompting proof. "If you are the Son of God." If it feels good – do it. If you think you are being treated unfairly – get angry. If you get caught in an awkward situation – lie. Temptation works by implication – "Is that really true?" Eve was lured by the same tactic (Genesis 3:1). The implication in the temptation was that God is a killjoy, a tyrant, an ogre – but it was all based on "if." If God is being unfair, if the fruit looks good for the taking – go for it. "You won't surely die," Satan insinuates later in the temptation scene.

Jesus resisted temptation. The "if" lost its power when Jesus deflected it by the greater power of God's Word. Jesus denied the devil the grounds for doubt to take root.

When we are tempted, ground yourself in the living Word, and ask yourself, "Where is that thought coming from?"

Suggested Song: "Leaning On the Everlasting Arms"

Pray: Loving God, guard and guide me when I face temptation. May I choose to listen to your word of truth, not the lies of the enemy of my soul. Thank you for our perfect example, in Jesus' name I pray, Amen.

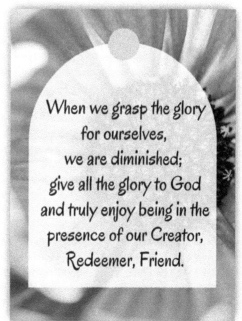

When we grasp the glory for ourselves, we are diminished; give all the glory to God and truly enjoy being in the presence of our Creator, Redeemer, Friend.

Meditation – Blessed

Praying Psalm 101: My theme song in life is your love, O God. I desire to live on the road of right living. We live in a world of injustice, prejudice, and inequality; you are the God of love and justice. I reject made-in-Canaan gods, I put a gag on gossip, and I associate with men and women on the straight and narrow, my eyes are on salt-of-the-earth people.

Scripture Text - Matthew 5:1-12

Blessed are the poor in spirit, for theirs is the kingdom of heaven. Matthew 5:3

The Beatitudes of Jesus are still perhaps the most familiar collection of teaching from the Bible. While religious memory has failed, a few words of Jesus still echo in the secular city: "Do unto others..." "Love one another..." "I am the way the truth and the life." And these eight blessings in their radically countercultural way are often acknowledged as good teaching from a good man. For those who follow Jesus as Lord, they are living blessings.

Jesus blesses us. A blessing was a familiar and accepted action from a religious leader in Jesus' day. Priests blessed the people in the name of God, rabbis spoke about God's blessing every time they read Psalm 1: "Blessed is the one ..."

We are blessed because Jesus sees us (verse 1). We are blessed because he calls us, teaches us, gives us a way to turn this world of pride, inequity, pleasure-seeking corruption on its head.

Receive his blessing today.

Suggested Song: "The Lord Bless You and Keep You"

Pray: Loving God, I receive your words of blessing today. Help me to grow more and more like Jesus, trusting and accepting the blessings you freely give. In Jesus' name, Amen.

Meditation – Anxiety

Praying Psalm 102: God, listen! Listen to my prayer, listen to the pain in my cries. Don't turn your back on me just when I need you so desperately. Pay attention. This is a cry for help! And hurry – this can't wait!

Scripture Text - Matthew 6: 25-34
But seek first his kingdom and his righteousness, and all these things will be given to you as well. Matthew 6:33

Years ago, I wrote these lyrics for a song called "Anxiety."
"In our society there's a commodity that doesn't need to be – it's anxiety.
People live with stress and unhappiness
because they fail to test God's faithfulness."
The refrain went, "Can you add another inch to your height by worrying? Can you say you'll be alive tomorrow night? There's no use worrying."
The emotional energy expended on worry is wasted. We could turn worry into worship, because when we worry, we are placing our confidence and wellbeing in something other than God. God alone deserves worth-ship. We should turn anxiety into intercession.
Jesus used two beautiful images from creation: birds of the air and flowers of the field. Their remarkable beauty and their total dependence on their Creator remind us of the foolishness of worry.
"People act as though they've got control of the way life goes.
Well, it's just not so.
Jesus taught his friends; anxiety ends when on him we depend."

Suggested Song: "Seek Ye First the Kingdom of God"

Pray: Heavenly Father, help me to look to the examples of creation – birds, trees, flowers and fauna to witness against your tender, nourishing care for your creatures – including me and my loved ones. In Jesus' name, Amen.

Relationship

Sometimes a resident would want to share about unresolved conflicts from the past. Betty shared with me about some long-time lingering challenges with her sibling. Ben told me about never feeling affirmed and appreciated by his father. Wanda had last seen her daughter almost ten years ago and they hadn't spoken since then. Relational tension is painful. Human beings are created to be in relationship. When these connections become frayed or severed it affects the very core of our beings. Mostly I would just listen to their experiences, sometimes asking a question to help them explore and unpack their pain. Occasionally they would find their way through to a desire to reach out for restoration and reconciliation. Listening and praying seemed to be of help.

Vein Glory, Amy

And So He Prospered

... and so he prospered
an epitaph coveted by most.
The two-stroke symmetry of seeking, working,
seeking, working... Seek - work.
Imbalance, inactivity if one aspect predominates.
With heavenly glance he balanced
active trust – a Two Part Invention.
This Spirit-walk truly mystifies.
We tried to do so much, so well
a model of goodness and faithfulness...
Reviving forgotten rites;
Calling for a return;
Administering justice;
Relying on a better battle-plan;
Repenting of death-bed pride
Hezekiah was tested and known by God ...
And so he prospered.

*"This is what Hezekiah did, doing what was good and faithful before the Lord his God...
He sought his God and worked wholeheartedly, and so he prospered."*

2 Chronicles 31:21

Meditation – All Authority

Praying Psalm 103: O my soul, bless the Lord, with all my strength I bless your holy name. You bless me and I don't take it for granted or forget it. You forgive my sins, heal my diseases, redeem me from hell, save me. Your love and mercy – a paradise crown. You renew my youth – bless you!

Scripture Text - Matthew 28:16-20
Then Jesus came to them and said, "All authority in heaven and on earth has been given to me." Matthew 28:18

Jesus frequently called his followers to mountains. In Matthew the text speaks of the Sermon on the Mount (Matthew 5-7). The Transfiguration of Jesus took place on a mountain (Matthew 17:1), the Mount of Olives was where Jesus spoke of last days (Matthew 24), and now as Jesus gave the disciples their mandate, the great commission, he called them to the mountain (Matthew 28:16). Jesus had a purpose in these mountaintop meetings. Firstly, they were remote places, away from the distractions and demands of the populace. Secondly, the air was clear, the view was spectacular, the perspective was fresh. A third reason might be to remind the followers of his authority – over people and over nature – the God of the mountains. A further reason was the significant role mountains played in figures like Abraham, Moses, Elijah and other prophetic greats. Now, with this declaration of his status, "All authority in heaven and on earth has been given to me," he sends the apostles to build his church.

Suggested Song: "Jesus Shall Reign"

Pray: Lord Jesus, I submit again to your authority in my life. Forgive me for trying to run things my own way. As I listen to your words of authority, I thank you for the privilege of being your witness. In Your name I pray, Amen.

Morning mist rising
in Easter Garden,
the third garden
- one long gone
- one yet to be

Meditation – Good News

Praying Psalm 104: God, my God, how great you are! Beautifully, gloriously robed, dressed up in sunlight. You are God of galaxies, wind, water, wild beasts, sardines, and sharks. Let me sing to you all my life long, hymns to you. Let my songs please you.

Scripture Text - Nahum 1:15-2:2

Look, there on the mountains, the feet of one who brings good news, who proclaims peace! Nahum 1:15

We live in a day when we are overwhelmed with news. If we allow ourselves, we can consume news from the moment we wake until we wearily drop into bed. TV, computer, smart phones, radio, print, social media – the bombardment rolls on. We hardly take time to allow one news item to settle in our ears before we hear the next. There is no peace.

Before we are ready to hear really good news, we must acknowledge the bad news: our sinful behaviour, racism, injustice, abuse, cruelty, and worst of all the bad news – our relational separation from God. Bad news. Then comes the sweet sound of a messenger of peace. The word of hope and wholeness. The promise of purpose and peace.

The Minor Prophet Nahum wrote a book of bad news for his day and yet, tucked almost midway through the gloom and doom, we are told to look! Listen! A good news messenger is walking this way. Good news.

Jesus says to us, *"Peace I leave with you; my peace I give you. I do not give to you as the world gives. Do not let your hearts be troubled and do not be afraid."* John 14:27.

Suggested Song: "Our God Reigns"

Pray: Heavenly Father, thank you for sending your son Jesus to be my Saviour. Thank you for the good news that my life is restored and I am a new creature in Christ. Thank you for good news. In Jesus' name, Amen.

Quiet Place, Corinne

Meditation – The Joy of the Lord

Praying Psalm 105: Hallelujah. Thank you, God. I will speak of your works, honour you, and I will keep my eyes open to watch for your works. You are a God of covenant. Forgive me for letting you down. You lead me from captivity and exile, singing for joy.

Scripture Text - Nehemiah 8:7-12
Nehemiah said, "Go and enjoy choice food and sweet drinks, and send some to those who have nothing prepared. This day is holy to our Lord. Do not grieve, for the joy of the LORD is your strength." Nehemiah 8:10

Parties, festivals, and community celebrations are markers that infuse the day-to-day with joy. We need them. The Bible is full of them. God wants humans to flourish, have deep joy and meaning in life. Nehemiah had made the people work hard in rebuilding the wall of Jerusalem. Now it was time to celebrate, not only because they had some time off, but at a deeper level, the word of the Law had been read and taught, the people were mourning their waywardness. Now Nehemiah says, "Go and enjoy ..." (verse 9).

Every day is a gift. Most mornings I join with others in the prayer, Lord, help me to live this day to the full. We will never experience these hours and opportunities in exactly the same way again. But some days are special, out of the ordinary – celebrate because the joy of the LORD is your strength.

Suggested Song: "The Joy of the Lord Is My Strength"

Pray: Loving God, thank you for the gift of this day. I choose to take joy in you and to acknowledge and accept your strength. In Jesus' name, Amen.

Through A Glass Darkly

Facing death is hard. We have fears, questions, and doubts. None of us relishes the possibility of physical pain and suffering. And then there are the spiritual battles. The enemy of our souls pesters and persists to the end. So, when Andy shared with me, "I'm not afraid to die, it's just the process I'm not looking forward to," I appreciated his honesty and courage. We talked about life after death. He had a deep and vibrant faith in Jesus. We imagined what it will be like to meet Jesus. We shared favourite inspirational poems and scripture, listened to music. Andy crossed over, and now he sees face-to-face, while we continue to see only through a glass darkly.

When A Dream Ends

When a dream ends
at night, we resume sleep; (usually)
When a dream ends
at morning, we wake and exchange realities.
When a dream ends
midday, we refocus and concentrate
our energies on the task.

When a vision ends
early in our life, we find a new one,
or not.
When a vision ends
midlife, we refocus, renew our energies
for the second half.

When a vision ends at death,
we pass on.
Pass on the dream
pass on the work
pass on the task
To new dreamers – visionaries.

Meditation – A Life Well-Lived

Praying Psalm 106: Thank you, God, for you are good, your love endures forever. Remember me, Lord, when you show favour to your people. You deliver your people again and again. Save us, Lord our God.

Scripture Text - Nehemiah 13:14-22

Then I commanded the Levites to purify themselves and go and guard the gates in order to keep the Sabbath day holy. Remember me for this also, my God, and show mercy to me according to your great love. Nehemiah 13:22

Four times the effective and faithful servant Nehemiah asks God to remember his efforts to live well (verses 14, 22, 29, 30), challenging the people of God to return to a true and vibrant spiritual life marked by purity, trust in God, and obedience to the teachings of God's Word. This was more than a rigid legalism on Nehemiah's part. The deeper concern was for holiness, devotion and encouraging the faithful to live their lives well before God.

God's design, as expressed in the law, commandments, and in the teachings of Jesus, is for humans to live faithfully and abundantly. The teachings are not punitive or petty, they are life-giving. As we grow in Christ, our daily desire is to embrace a life well-lived. Our culture tells us that a good life is reflected in our salary, prestige, possessions, power, and popularity. We are called to be faithful followers of Jesus. We also pray with Nehemiah, "Remember me with favour, my God."

WHAT CAN BE DONE IN THE TIME OF TERROR? A COLLISION OF CONSEQUENCES.

Suggested Song: "Trust and Obey"

Pray: Remember me, dear God, for the life I seek to live in your strength, grace and favour, in Jesus' name, Amen.

Meditation – Face to Face

Praying Psalm 107: I love to tell the story of your love, faithfulness, goodness, and redemption. People stray from you in so many ways; guard and guide my steps. You turn deserts into pools of water, parched ground into flowering springs. You feed the hungry, provide a good harvest, place the homeless in cities of support. I long to be wise – I will heed these things and ponder your loving deeds, Lord.

Scripture Text - Numbers 6:22-27
The LORD turn his face toward you and give you peace. Numbers 6:26

In conversation, appropriate eye contact is very meaningful. Eyes, it is said, are the window to the soul. When we make eye contact with someone, we get a better sense of their mood and meaning than when we just hear them speak, or read their thoughts in writing. So much inflection, nuance and innuendo are deciphered by face-to-face communication.

This familiar Aaronic blessing from Numbers 6 speaks of God's face being turned toward us, shining on us. What a beautiful image. When a loving father or mother looks with approval and affirmation on their child, the bond is transforming.

A gospel song says, "Face to face with Christ my saviour, face to face – what will it be – when with rapture I behold Him, Jesus Christ who died for me."

I once had a pastor who encouraged us as a congregation to look at him while he spoke this Aaronic blessing over us. He explained that a blessing was a good word to be received from God with gladness and peace, with our eyes wide open.

Suggested Song:
"Turn Your Eyes Upon Jesus"

Pray: Loving Father, thank you for this blessing of peace and intimacy with you, my creator, sustainer, saviour, and friend. May your spirit fill me as I live today, in Jesus' name, Amen.

Lighthouse, Ursula

Meditation – Your Kingdom

Praying Psalm 108: My heart is confident in you, O God. No wonder I can sing your praise with all my heart. For your unfailing love is higher than the heavens. Your faithfulness reaches to the clouds. Be exalted!

Scripture Text - Obadiah 1:19-21
Deliverers will go up on Mount Zion to govern the mountains of Esau. And the kingdom will be the LORD's. Obadiah 21

Jesus taught us as his followers to pray, "Your kingdom come on earth as it is in heaven." (Matthew 6:10) A kingdom is a realm, a territory, a designated sphere of influence. The people of Israel were on promised land. The symbol of land is important in many, but not all cultures. The underlying reality is always that the land belonged ultimately to the sovereign Lord. We are stewards and dwellers in the land, but the earth is the Lord's (Psalm 24:1).

When the prophet Obadiah speaks to "this company of Israelite exiles" (verse 20), saying they will possess the land, it is a word of hope and promise. The image of promised land for our eternal destiny in the presence of God expresses an even deeper, truer hope. Our great, eternal hope.

We keep praying for God's will to be done – in our personal lives, and in our world – for his kingdom to come daily, increasingly, for the kingdom is the Lord's.

Suggested Song: "This Is My Father's World"

Pray: Our Father in heaven, hallowed be your name, your kingdom come, your will be done, on earth as it is in heaven. Give us today our daily bread. And forgive us our sins, as we also have forgiven those who sin against us. And lead us not into temptation but deliver us from the evil one. In Jesus' name, Amen.

We Will Remember

Memorial services for residents at Tabor Home and Valhaven provide opportunities to support family members, and to give staff a chance to pay their respects. A picture of the departed loved one is shown, and a brief life-story shared. Sometimes a friend or family member says a few words. It was beautiful to hear residents like Don or Erika reading, "At the rising of the sun and at its going down, at the rustling of the leaves and in the beauty of autumn, at the blowing of the wind and in the chill of winter, at the opening of the buds and in the rebirth of spring, at the blueness of the skies and in the warmth of summer – we will remember."

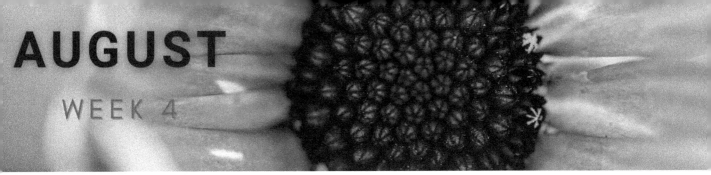

Three Haiku From Those Who Watched

The women stood near
Weeping for themselves and Him
The mothers mothered.

Leg-breaking soldiers
Finding Him dead, pierced for good.
Blood and water flow.

Joseph cared for Him
Rich Arimathean love.
Josephs – start to end.

Meditation – Living Stones

Praying Psalm 109: O God whom I praise, don't stand silent and aloof when others attack. Deal well with me, O sovereign Lord, for the sake of your reputation. Rescue me because you are so faithful and good. You stand beside the needy, ready to save them from those who would condemn them.

Scripture Text - 1 Peter 2:4-10

You also, like living stones, are being built into a spiritual house to be a holy priesthood, offering spiritual sacrifices acceptable to God through Jesus Christ.
1 Peter 2:5

"Living stones" is a vivid, almost paradoxical image to represent the church. We see magnificent cathedrals and churches built to the glory of God. We marvel at the architectural beauty, the craftsmanship, the interplay of light and texture. Peter implies that as fine as these structures may be, as believers in Jesus, as his chosen, precious people, we come alive as living temples. We come alive as we are built by God's hand, the great Architect, into a spiritual house. Stones have solidity, strength, stability. Simon the fisherman was nicknamed by Jesus, "The Rock." We fit together in a living, growing, organic house of God.

In bygone days the church spire was the highest building in the village. Then it was surpassed by a city hall or an office tower. Now it is our shopping mall that centres our towns. While this may sadden us as believers, falsely making us think the church has lost its central place, remember – we are living stones – reflecting the life and dynamic of the Living Stone, the cornerstone, Jesus Christ.

Suggested Song:
"The Church's One Foundation"

Pray: Thank you, Jesus, that we are alive in you, our living Stone, raised from the dead and seated at the Father's right hand.
In your mercy, let us live for you today, in your name, Amen.

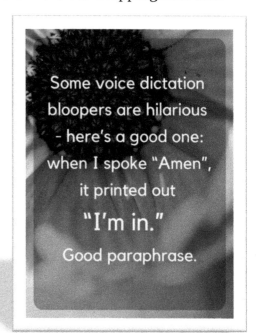

Some voice dictation bloopers are hilarious - here's a good one: when I spoke "Amen", it printed out **"I'm in."** Good paraphrase.

Meditation – Oh Lord, It's Hard to Be Humble

Praying Psalm 110: Lord, you protect, preserve, and prosper those leaders who rely on you. You are the one who grants and extends power, you stand at the right hand, protecting and preserving. You provide refreshment to leaders from brooks along the way.

Scripture Text - 1 Peter 5:5-11
Humble yourselves, therefore, under God's mighty hand, that he may lift you up in due time. 1 Peter 5:6

The old country song amusingly twangs, "Oh Lord, it's hard to be humble – when you're perfect in every way!" We chuckle perhaps, but it has a truth. It is hard to be humble, for the moment we think we've achieved it, we've lost it. It's like the braggarts who are so proud of their humility award.

One approach to humility is not to think less of ourselves, but to think of ourselves less. Another suggestion is that humility is knowing and filling our appropriate, God-given space. No higher – no lower. It is not grovelling, like Charles Dickens' fictional character Uriah Heep.

The text says to humble ourselves "under God's mighty hand." As we recognize and worship God as God, we recognize and welcome that we are not God. It is the proper perspective.

The word, "humble," derives from the word we use for soil, "humus." We are not to think of ourselves or others as dirt, rather as living, vibrant, healthy soil in which the Lord can plant his good seed.

Suggested Song: "May the Mind of Christ My Saviour"

Pray: Father, Son, and Holy Spirit, live and move through me today as I seek to live in right relationship under you, in Jesus' name, Amen.

Meditation – *Curriculum Vitae*

Praying Psalm 111: With all my heart I thank you, Lord. As I worship you in church, I acknowledge again how amazing are your deeds. Your never-failing righteousness, glory, majesty, the wonders performed in history and in my life. Your name is awe- inspiring.
I am in holy fear, reverence, and submission before you – forever!

Scripture Text - 2 Peter 1:3-8
For if you possess these qualities in increasing measure, they will keep you from being ineffective and unproductive in your knowledge of our Lord Jesus Christ. 2 Peter 1:8

We all assemble life resumes. Sometimes called a *curriculum vitae* (CV) which reflects the course or curriculum of a life – our life. Usually, this CV includes training and education, work experiences and special accomplishments. Hopefully, when we look over our life resumes, we can see all the ways we faithfully followed God.

The apostle Peter provides an impressive collage of character traits we should all have in our resumes: goodness, knowledge, self-control, perseverance, godliness, mutual affection, and love. A similar list is provided by Paul, described as fruit of the spirit (Galatians 5:22-23), but this fruit is planted and nurtured by the Holy Spirit. The character curricula of our text are things we "make every effort to add" to our life-resume.

If every Christian were working on and working out these seven spiritual signposts, the world would be transformed. Lord, may it be so. May we be effective and productive in our life with Jesus Christ our Lord.

Suggested Song: "Take My Life and Let It Be Consecrated"

Pray: Thank you, Father, for the many good experiences you bring into my life that create a curriculum of godliness. Today, please use me for your glory, in Jesus' name, Amen.

Homing Instinct

"I want to go home." Every time her loved one came to visit, they were greeted with Lydia's sad refrain. For her, home was with her parents back on the prairies. We are wired with a homing-instinct. If it is true that the purpose of human life is "To glorify God and enjoy him forever," as the Westminster Shorter Catechism declares, then no wonder we want to go home. The ancient shepherd song says, *"Surely goodness and mercy shall follow me all the days of my life, and I will dwell in the house of the Lord forever."* (Psalm 23:6) Soon Lydia, very soon.

Praying Psalm 112: I reverence and fear you, Lord, and delight in obeying your commands. Please bless my family. May this next generation be godly and bless those around them. I try to be generous, honest, fair, trusting in your providence. May we share freely and give generously to those in need.

Roots, Ray

FALL

September – November

All the Laughter and Life

All the laughter and life,
sunshine and warm warped waves
of turquoise and starlight
will fade, will transform
will be transfigured to a new earth
with sea of glass and a throne translucent.

Then there will be new songs
from every tribe, nation, ethnic flavours
new world savours
after our earth-born labours.
Ushering us to our new home
in our new world with our new bodies
our new work.

Maybe it will be continuation, extension,
perfection of this earthly vocation
singer, speaker, shepherd, teacher,
gardener, word-player, scribbler,
or it will be something entirely new
and unrehearsed – true improv.

"The dead will hear the voice of the son of God and those who hear will live." *
Listen, listen
beyond all the laughter and life, moaning, strife
to hear the warm waves of the Voice.

*John 5:25

Meditation – Costly

⛬ **Praying Psalm 113:** I am your servant, Lord, receive my praise, blessings, glory, and worship. Who can compare with you? You lift up the poor from the dust and the needy from the garbage dump. You place the lonely in families.

📖 **Scripture Text** - Philemon 17-21
If he has done you any wrong or owes you anything, charge it to me. Philemon 18

If someone were to ask you, "What does it cost to be a Christian," how would you answer? If you responded by saying, "Becoming a Christian is free, it is a gift, there is no price we could pay for it because salvation is offered freely," you would be correct. And if you answered, "Being a Christian will cost you everything – we lay down our life for Christ and serve others sacrificially, we give of our resources, and we do this freely and gladly," you would also be correct. Our faith is free, and it costs everything.

The Apostle Paul was reinstating a slave who had escaped from his master Philemon. Paul writes a letter of reference for this newborn former slave Onesimus, urging Philemon to forgive him, accept him, and realize that he is no longer a slave (verse 16). Further, Paul offers to pay any outstanding wrongs or debts owing. "Charge it to me." This is costly discipleship. Risky leadership, and godly friendship.

🎵 **Suggested Song:** "Freely"

🙏 **Pray:** Loving Heavenly Father, thank you for saving me and paying the ransom for my sins. Following Jesus is costly. Jesus modelled the cost in laying down his life for us, for his friends. Help me serve others with that kind of sacrificial love, in Jesus' name, Amen.

The call of I AM at the burning bush banished Moses from desert exile.

Meditation – Great Expectations

Praying Psalm 114: When Israel escaped from Egypt, when they left that foreign land, the promised land of Judah became your sanctuary, your kingdom. The Red Sea got out of their way, Jordan turned aside, mountains skipped, hills frolicked, tremble, O earth, at the presence of the Lord.

Scripture Text - Philippians 1:18b-21

I eagerly expect and hope that I will in no way be ashamed, but will have sufficient courage so that now as always Christ will be exalted in my body, whether by life or by death. Philippians 1:20

We all need a reason to get up in the morning. Among members of populations who have enjoyed long lives, when asked their wisdom, they often answer, "Have something in your day to look forward to." Expectation, hope, anticipation, energizes and motivates us. It may be a large event or project, but more often it is something simple and small. Enjoying a meal with someone you love, going for a walk, talking to a friend you haven't seen for a while, reading an engaging book or article. Whatever gives joy, purpose, and a reason to move forward.

As Christians we have many more reasons for expectations and hope. Paul writes to the church in Philippi expressing his confidence that God is using and will use his life to exalt Jesus Christ. This assurance is because he knows the church is praying for him as he endures life in prison. As we rely on prayer, and as we faithfully pray for others, we can gain courage and have purpose in living our lives to the glory of Jesus. This applies in this life and into the next – for to live is Christ and to die is gain (verse 21).

Suggested Song:
"Higher Ground"

Pray: Loving God, thank you for the gift of this day. May I live fully in your joy and presence as I serve, love, and grow in you. I look to you for purpose, in Jesus' name, Amen.

Nicola Valley Vista, Ray

Meditation – What A Wonderful World

Praying Psalm 115: Not to us, O Lord, not to me, but to your name goes all the glory. Grant me prudence to keep my eyes off speechless, blind, senseless idols. I trust in you. Remember me, bless my children. I praise you always.

Scripture Text – Philippians 2:1-4
Do nothing out of selfish ambition or vain conceit. Rather, in humility value others above yourselves. Philippians 2:3

If we are honest, we must admit we are self-obsessed creatures. Self-centred, self-helping, self-improvement, self-satisfied, and the list could go on. Some would argue that it is part of an evolutionary process of survival of the fittest. If we don't look after ourselves, our best interests, our desires and self-preservation, nobody else will.

Occasionally we encounter someone who is genuinely selfless. My mother-in-law was such a person. She put the needs and wellbeing of her husband, children, and grandchildren before her own. She was also one of the most truly joyful people I knew. She didn't have an easy childhood, and in her young adult years she helped her mother after her father had died. She was a blessing to those in her life, including me.

We are called as followers of Jesus, our Master who laid down his life for us, to set aside selfish modes of being, to have an honest opinion of ourselves, not inflated by pride or selfish ambition. We are called to value others above ourselves. What a wonderful world that would be!

Suggested Song: "Make Me A Blessing"

Pray: Loving Father, forgive my selfishness. Help me set aside my conceit and vanity, and replace it with the desire to bless others, in Jesus' name, Amen.

When a Symbol Expires

The "evergreen" tree died... Tabor had placed a living evergreen tree on the front porch of the Home as a statement of hope, light, promise, and legacy. It looked beautiful in the cold months of December and January 2020-21. It was being watered regularly, the staff said, but by March it was looking tired. When Ken and I went to move it for planting in Cherry Lane Garden, it was like the Charlie Brown Christmas tree, shivering its needles all over the concrete. We checked to see if there was green showing under the bark, a hopeful spark of life. It was in bad shape. We planted it anyway, pampering it with good, rich soil and plenty of water, and hoping for the best. It died. Was its death a bad omen, or an object lesson reminding us that to everything there is "a time to live and a time to die?"

Humour Me

Humour me as I reflect on dirt:
humus, in its Latinate
compost, in its degraded state
soil, in its growing form
dirt to those who only see
the earth beneath their feet
all terms for home for worms
and microbial, bacterial, ingestive,
digestive decay for a future day.

The process is slow silent invisible
like the germination of humility,
the breakdown is relentless, but with a purpose,
just like the goal of humility.

There is heat, earthy smells and wiggly things
it's sometimes not a pleasant process.
Leaves left alone in contact with
soil, elements of sun, wind, rain
decay through worms,
though worms destroy this body...

Yet broken down to baser humbler form
it becomes of value – rich black gold
Gardener's delight.

Meditation – Troubles of the World

Praying Psalm 116: I love you, Lord, because you heard my voice and my prayer for mercy. I will pray as long as I have breath! You protect those of childlike faith. I will lift up a cup of salvation and praise you for saving me.

Scripture Text – Philippians 4:4-9

Do not be anxious about anything, but in every situation, by prayer and petition, with thanksgiving, present your requests to God. Philippians 4:6

Every generation experiences looming societal threats and challenges. Ours happens to include climate change, pandemic, and racial injustice. Previous generations faced world wars, threat of nuclear destruction, and racial intolerance. In Jesus' time, two thousand years ago, people feared ruthless empires and crazy emperors, starvation, plagues, and racial targeting. Sadly, some things never change.

Jesus said, "each day has enough trouble of its own" (Matthew 6:34), his point being, don't project and anticipate tomorrow's problems. This only increases anxiety.

The Apostle Paul advises turning our worries into worship, our problems into prayer. "Rejoice in the Lord" is to worship and trust our Heavenly Father. When we pray, we take our eyes off our own situation and bring our worries and anxiety to God. When we petition God, we acknowledge that God is sovereign and in control, and we are not. And when we give thanks, our anxiety can be transformed to praise. Pray first, pray faithfully, pray fervently. and the peace of God which is beyond human understanding will guard us, in Christ Jesus.

Suggested Song: "I Need Thee Every Hour"

Pray: Heavenly Father, I admit that I feel overwhelmed sometimes by the pressures, pain, and problems of this world. Help me today as I pray for your peace, in Christ Jesus' holy name, Amen.

"Mandate Freedom!"
I guess some
don't see the
paradox.

Meditation – No Foolin'

Praying Psalm 117: All nations will praise you. Your unfailing love endures forever. I praise you!

Scripture Text - Proverbs 1:1-7
The fear of the LORD is the beginning of knowledge, but fools despise wisdom and instruction. Proverbs 1:7

Do you love to learn? Maybe this seems weird to some, but if I could be a lifelong student, attending lectures and studying, I would be happy. I love university campuses. When I travel to a city, I enjoy walking the grounds and gardens, appreciating the trees and plants, the architecture, the vibe. My wife jokingly says that I could indeed be a lifelong student.

Our text says some folks despise wisdom and instruction. Proverbs is not referring to formal education, attending lectures, searching libraries, writing essays. Rather, the writer means we are fools when we don't humble ourselves, acknowledge that we are lacking wisdom, and fear God enough to ask for it. Reverence, respect, awe, and faithful obedience is what it looks like to fear the living God.

Most of our formal education we receive when we are young. The young are often more open to learning. And many of our life-lessons we learn as we age. We must keep learning. Jesus says, unless we come to him as children, open to listen and learn, we will not enter the kingdom. Let's live and learn like children, not like fools who despise instruction.

Suggested Song: "Children of the Heavenly Father"

Pray: Loving Heavenly Father, I come to you in worship, reverence and awe, knowing that you love to teach me your ways. Help me to live more like your beloved son, Jesus, in whose name I pray, Amen.

Meditation – Knowing God

Praying Psalm 118: You are good – your love endures forever (repeat 3 times). You have made the Stone the builders rejected to become the cornerstone; you did this and it is marvellous. Lord, save us! Lord, grant us success! You are my God, and I will praise you.

Scripture Text - Proverbs 2:1-5
Then you will understand the fear of the LORD and find the knowledge of God.
Proverbs 2:5

By my count, the four verses of Proverbs 2:1-4 have seven encouragements relating to finding "the knowledge of God" (verse 5). They begin with "if you...", then list the actions, "accept and store up," "pay attention (turn your ear)," "apply yourself to understanding," "ask for insight," "urgently seek (call out)," "look for it" (like silver)," "search for it (like treasure)." Hebrew poetry uses a method of artistic repetition called parallelism. The author of this text is piling up the admonitions and exhortations to seek for understanding. All these encouragements, and all our actions, are not to acquire head-knowledge, but heart-relationship.

There are many things we search for in life. A sense of personal purpose, being in close relationships with loved ones, a satisfying and meaningful life. These are all good things. But if you seek, the writer of Proverbs says, you will find and know God.

Jesus also says, "Seek and you will find ..."

Suggested Song: "Seek Ye First"

Pray: Lord God, forgive me for seeking lesser things. Today I seek to know you more, and to love you deeply. Thank you for knowing me, in Jesus' name, Amen.

Vocation

Staff commitment and steadfast service through the worst of times is inspirational. They are true heroes. Caring and serving and coming to know and love each tenant, each resident, is part of the vocation. It's no vacation! It is truly a calling to care from the heart. The tensions of being short-staffed due to illness during the pandemic exerted huge stress on everyone. Meeting and briefly talking with staff in the halls or at their station, I could hear the fatigue and frustration, but they persevered despite obstacles and challenges. The human spirit is an amazingly resilient, responsive entity. Pressing on for months and eventually years takes its toll. Sickness, resignations, and discouragements were part of the journey through the pandemic. And as our world enters new phases of virus-spread and measures to bring things to a new normal, we sometimes grow weary in doing good. Then Sally had a new grandbaby. Tim recovered from a lengthy illness. Bob's daughter got married. And hope returns.

Curious Climber, Ursula

The Crown of History

Sing a song of proclamation
Of great deeds and events
Set in the crown of history.
Sung by mighty monarch
With a strong hillside lyric voice
Of a shepherd, accompanied by
Harp, lyre, and cymbal.

The whole earth will hear this song
and be drawn, wooed to One
Who does amazing things
Every day; today and long ago
And yet to come.

The Roman Empire heard it
During census-taking time
In hillside harmony
(Premiered for a few select shepherds)
And one day all will hear
the distant triumph song
and bend the knee.

Meditation – Generosity

Praying Psalm 119: Lord, in this A-Z poem of prayer and praise, I again commit myself to obey your way, law, statutes, precepts, decrees, commands, words, counsels, and promises. Let me live that I might praise you, and let your law sustain me.

Scripture Text - Proverbs 11:24-26
One person gives freely, yet gains even more; another withholds unduly, but comes to poverty. Proverbs 11:24

God has created the world with a fundamental principle of abundance. When I take a seed pod from a plant and look carefully at the profusion of potential life contained in a single pod, I see abundance. When I look at the stars, beyond counting, I see God's outpoured generosity. When I think of the kingdom principle of sowing and sharing the good news of Jesus, I see the principle of generosity.

I have a reminder on my day timer for every day at 11:24 A.M. It reminds me of this call in Proverbs 11:24, to live, give, think generously. The principle applies to money, time, love – when we are miserly, we never have enough, when we give freely, we gain even more. I had a friend who said, "You can't outgive God."

Jesus humbled himself, taking the form of a servant, and offered his life for me (Philippians 2). If that is not the extreme evidence of a generous God, what is? Why would we "withhold unduly?"

Suggested Song: "Freely, Freely"

Pray: Heavenly Father, you are a generous God. Thank you for your many blessings. Help me to live and give generously, in Jesus' name, Amen.

EVEN GOOD THINGS CAN BECOME A SNARE. LOOK UP "NEHUSHTAN."

Meditation – Soothing Words

Praying Psalm 120: In my distress I called on you and you heard me. Save me, release me, use me. I am for peace; but everyone around me wants war!

Scripture Text - Proverbs 15:1-7
The soothing tongue is a tree of life, but a perverse tongue crushes the spirit. Proverbs 15:4

Our words have great impact. When we say unkind things to anyone it leaves an impression. Sometimes we can dismiss the comment as coming from someone who needs extra grace, but when it comes from a loved one, a parent, a spouse, a sibling, a colleague, the words wound.

The series of proverbs in Proverbs 15:1-7 mostly deal with our speech. The writer encourages "gentle answers," speech that adorns, that soothes, and speaks truth and wisdom. In contrast, the harsh word, the mouth gushing folly, the twisted or perverted or cutting words bring anger and injury.

The image of a soothing tongue being like a tree of life is a beautiful picture of healing, wellness, fruitfulness, and a sweet aroma. Life-giving.

Think of the people in your life today. If we decided to make every word that we speak to them be words of life, not diminishment, of healing, not wounding, of soothing and assuring, not of agitation and aggravation, our words and our lives will bring life and hope.

Suggested Song: "Wonderful Words of Life"

Pray: Loving God of all grace, help us to speak words of fruitfulness and freshness today, being kind in word and deed, in Jesus' name, Amen.

Coastline, Amy

Meditation – Blessed

Praying Psalm 121: My help comes from you, Lord, maker of heaven and earth. You watch me, guide me, help me, protect me. You watch over my life, my coming and going both now and forevermore.

Scripture Text - Psalm 1

Blessed is the one who does not walk in step with the wicked or stand in the way that sinners take or sit in the company of mockers. Psalm 1:1

The Bible is full of blessings. The priests were taught to bless with the words, "The Lord bless you and keep you." The Patriarchs offered blessings to their children and families. Jesus spoke blessings in the Beatitudes. We might replace the biblical Word with other day-to-day synonyms like, "I hope your day goes well" or "all the best" or "live long and prosper." Psalm 1 speaks of blessings resulting from specific choices a person makes. Choosing to walk through our day with uplifting attitudes, to stand alongside those who want to make a positive difference in their world, to spend time with encouragers.

Blessings flow from good choices.

Bad choices lead to a dead end. Specks in the wind.

This first psalm in the prayer book we call Psalms is like a portal, a doorway to full, flourishing life. It includes warning and welcome, correction and capacity.

The first word – blessed, if one chooses well.

Suggested Song: "Showers of Blessing"

Pray: Heavenly Father, help me make good choices today, so that I may live under your blessing and share that wellbeing with everyone I meet. In Jesus' name, Amen.

Praying For Miracles

I am frequently blessed, and sometimes challenged, by the brief conversations I have with tenants following a Sunday service. Often it is a word of thanks or affirmation. Sometimes it is a question or observation based on something I said in the meditation. One such exchange was with Wilmer after Transfiguration Sunday. I had spoken about the appearance of Moses and Elijah on the mountain, and how they spoke of Jesus' upcoming exodus. Wilmer observed, "Moses and Elijah – word and miracles. We don't believe God can do miracles these days. The church doesn't pray for miracles anymore. God is more than willing and is all-powerful." A good word. A good reminder. I have been praying for miracles these days.

Glass Darkly

Glass is a good simile
"The lake is like glass this morning."
Glowing, luminous, still, silvery
As clear as glass, motionless, reflective.
Yet glass is only motionless to the naked eye.
Molecules moving at invisible speed
While moving lake water glides, shifts, and flows.
With eyes to see would the fixed pane
Also flow, glow with liquid motion?
Like in its furnace-phase, molten
now cool, hard, fragile-firm.
Old windows have that warp undulating
plane. More like lake surface.
They have seen more calm sunrises
and glowing golden refracted sunsets;
windows of gold in mansions across the lake – always on the other side.
Soon the morning gusts will ripple,
reconfigure the glass reflector.
A different simile will be a descriptor:
      like shining diamonds, like white-capped dancers
      like ribs or mountain ridges
      like valleys deep in wind-swept,
      wind-whipped surface.
Glass is a good metaphor:
"Now we see through a glass darkly"
Reflections, but warped and waving,
waiting through perfect pain
to see face to face
and know as we are known.

Meditation – LORD, LORD

Praying Psalm 122: I rejoice with other pilgrims who say, "Let's go to the house of the Lord." We pray for peace, and the security of those who love you. Thank you for the peace you provide for family and friends.

Scripture Text - Psalm 8

LORD, our Lord, how majestic is your name in all the earth! You have set your glory in the heavens. Psalm 8:1

God is immeasurably beyond our human comprehension.

God is as close to us as our next breath. LORD ... our LORD, reminds me of Jesus' prayer, "Our Father ... in heaven."
Expansive and intimate. Awesome and incarnate in Jesus. Grand and personal. Even infants know to praise God, and Jesus welcomed the children. The universe speaks of his inexpressible glory, and we also are invited to join the party of praise. We are amazing creatures – we are dust. We have a mandate to steward the good things of God's glory, in a way that shows complete trust and dependence.

This psalm is set to inspiring music, and it quietly graces one of my favourite teacups!

Compassionate LORD even our grandchildren coo your Name.

Creator King, the galaxies gust Your GLORY.

Why do You even take notice of us? Why have You granted us dominion? Majestic, Awesome is Your Name.

Suggested Song: "O Lord, Our Lord How Majestic Is Your Name"

Pray: I worship and praise you for your majestic greatness and your loving intimacy, O LORD, my Lord. In Jesus' name, Amen.

Watching swallows dip and touch the surface of the pond makes me realize how little and skimming is my knowledge of the love of God.

Meditation – Restored

Praying Psalm 123: I lift my eyes to you, to you who sits on the throne of heaven. As the eyes of slaves look to those they serve, so my eyes look to you. Have mercy on us, Lord, have mercy. We have endured contempt.

Scripture Text - Psalm 51:1-2, 7-12
Create in me a pure heart, O God, and renew a steadfast spirit within me. Psalm 51:10

Our Creator God keeps on creating. Our text asks God to "create in me a pure heart." Our "heart" represent the centre of our emotions, our wills, our passions, and pursuits. God continues his good work of creation in our hearts, at our invitation.

The word "sin" is unpopular these days. When we miss the intended target of living in ways that please God, we sin. Psalm 51 is a lament and plea of David for mercy, cleansing, renewal, particularly considering his recent sins (2 Samuel 11).

Our confidence of receiving pardon and restoration of joy is our loving God's unfailing love and compassion (verse 1).

This amazing grace is offered to us by God because we are his creation. God looks at creation and says, that is good, so a way is made for us, through the loving sacrifice of Jesus, to be remade, reborn, recreated in the image of Jesus. Amazing Creator! Amazing Saviour!

Suggested Song: "Amazing Grace"

Pray: Loving God, restore me today. Wash all my sin away, renew, refresh, forgive and cleanse me for your glory and my salvation, in Jesus' name, Amen.

In a Pig's Eye, Amy

Meditation – Flourish

Praying Psalm 124: You are on our side, against enemies, because we trust you. We praise you for protection. We have escaped like a bird from a snare. Our help is in the name of the Lord, the maker of heaven and earth.

Scripture Text - Psalm 92:12-15
The righteous will flourish like a palm tree, they will grow like a cedar of Lebanon.
Psalm 92:12

The word "flourish" expresses abundance, health, fullness, flowering. In the garden, we choose a good site, rich soil, sufficient nutrients, and provide adequate water, all in the desire to have a flourishing plant. When we see a plant withering and suffering, we seek a diagnosis and remedy. The desired outcome is health and wellbeing.

Our children need love, acceptance, nurture, and training to provide ideal conditions for flourishing. In our spiritual lives we seek rightness and relatedness to God and to others to live in ways that produce wellbeing and productivity. Jesus said he came that we might have life to the full. Abundant. Flourishing.

God's word is saturated with the call and equipping to live a righteous life. Spending time with God through prayer and listening to the Word, loving others as Jesus loves, forgiving and being forgiven. These are all conditions for healthy, flourishing lives, staying fresh and green – at any age (verse 14).

Suggested Song: "Simply Trusting"

Pray: Loving God, through the saving work of Jesus and empowering work of the Holy Spirit I thank you that I can flourish in you today, in Jesus' name, Amen.

Just Have To Dance

Seeing the joy and renewed energy in the face and movement of Heather, a kind and supportive care aide, was uplifting for me. I had brought my guitar into Cherry Lane that afternoon and Heather was walking hand in hand with Edna. When Edna heard me playing "He's Got the Whole World in His Hands" on the guitar, she started to dance. Heather lit up. She said, "Edna, what a beautiful dance! You love this song." Some days are more challenging than others. Sometimes it's hard at work not to just go through the motions. But when a moment of genuine and unexpected joy breaks in – well – you just have to dance!

Resin To Embalm

Myrrh provides resin to embalm,
Mask the death stench
With aroma of pungent perfume.
Admire a newborn King
With this gift of death?
Blur of life and death
Burial rites; burial rights.

Myrrh provides reason for travel
Common currency of caravan trader
Aroma sent to appease and please
The dimmed and dying sense.

Myrrh provides risen body
With cologne for the Emmaus walk
Scent to be recognized
Sent to break bread with companions.

Wrapped in cloth like travelling bread
In the house of bread – Bethlehem
Rising brings the fresh bread of Life
The fresh breath of air – maritime sea breeze.
Reason for resin, rising.

Meditation – Author

Praying Psalm 125: I trust in you – you mighty Mountain – you cannot be shaken but endure forever. Thank you for all your gifts, keep us from evil. I want to live right before you and know your peace.

Scripture Text - Revelation 1:4-8

"I am the Alpha and the Omega," says the Lord God, "who is, and who was, and who is to come, the Almighty." Revelation 1:8

I love to read good books. I have many favourite authors, I have read and collected their works over many decades. I started reading seriously in my late teens. C. S. Lewis, Francis Schaeffer, J. R. R. Tolkien, and John Stott were some of my earliest and still ongoing reading friends. My wife says my bookshelves are lined with my "friends."

Authors express their ideas and personalities through words. They carefully craft sentences. They string these together in paragraphs which form chapters. Each word is significant on its own, and its purpose is to lead us to a point of awareness, of knowledge and joy, and ultimately to enrichment.

Our divine Author uses the letters of the Greek alphabet, the building blocks of words in self-reference. The Alpha and the Omega. God encompasses the A-Z of all reality and potential.

At the centre of the word "authority" is "author." Who is the author of my life? In both the sense of origin and of orientation. God is the true Author entitled to all authority. God has created a good book. A true friend. Shelf-less.

Suggested Song:
"To God Be the Glory"

Pray: Loving God, you are the author and authority of my life. I choose to submit again to your restoring and re-storying work in my life today, in Jesus' name, Amen.

— 66 —
Sing praise to God, connecting breath, vocal cords, spirit and Spirit.
— 99 —

Meditation – Worthy

Praying Psalm 126: Lord, make the dream true again: bring me back from exile. Fill me with laughter, singing, joy. Restore me like a stream in the desert. Tears to harvest, singing for weeping.

Scripture Text - Revelation 5:8-13
Worthy is the Lamb, who was slain, to receive power and wealth and wisdom and strength and honor and glory and praise! Revelation 5:12

The English word "worship" comes from worth-ship. The question we must daily ask ourselves is who or what has ultimate worth in our life? There are many worthy things in this life: worthy pursuits like building beautiful relationships, creating inspiring art, leading and serving others; there are worthy experiences like a glorious sunrise or sunset, an uplifting piece of music, a reflective poem; but none of these worthy things should take the central place of worth-ship in our life.

Adding the suffix "ship" to a word implies direction, guidance, empowering. Like friend-ship, leader-ship, owner-ship. What we worth-ship is what gives us direction and purpose, it carries us (like a ship).

When we worship Jesus, the Lamb who offered his life to pay for our sins, we acknowledge that He alone is worthy. So, we humbly, thankfully acknowledge his power, wealth, wisdom, and strength.

Suggested Song: "Thou Art Worthy"

Pray: Lord of all, accept my praise and worship today, for you alone are worthy, in Jesus' name, Amen.

Tranquil Estate, Ursula

Meditation – Home

Praying Psalm 127: Unless you build it, Lord, I waste my time. Unless you protect, Lord, my feeble attempts to guard will be futile. Thank you for our children and grandchildren. A gift from you, a blessing.

Scripture Text - Revelation 21:1-4
And I heard a loud voice from the throne saying, "Look! God's dwelling place is now among the people, and he will dwell with them. They will be his people, and God himself will be with them and be their God." Revelation 21:3

My memories of my childhood home are warm and happy. I fully and sadly acknowledge that not everyone's home was a good place. But let's imagine a perfect, ideal home, where there is warmth, love, nurture, and acceptance. The Bible speaks much about home. Often the image of home indicates being in the presence and love of God. *"I will dwell in the house of the LORD forever."* (Psalm 23:6) *"Lord, you have been our dwelling place throughout all generations."* (Psalm 90:1) *"My Father's house has many rooms; I will come back and take you to be with me that you also may be where I am."* (John 14:2)

We don't know all the details of life after death, but the Bible provides many beautiful images and pictures to encourage and give hope and perseverance to remain faithful. To me, one of the most powerful images for life in God's presence is "home." We will be in the very presence of God, and we will know warmth, love, and goodness, forever (John 14:3).

Suggested Song: "Surely Goodness and Mercy"

Pray: Father in heaven, you are preparing a home for me, where I will be in your presence forever – glory! For today, help me live faithfully and obediently for you as you bring your kingdom. In Jesus' name, Amen.

The Weariness In Doing Well

I enjoy interacting with staff doing their daily job. Sometimes I pop my head into the kitchen door to ask how everyone is doing, to comment on the lovely smells of lunch being prepared, and to thank them for their good work. As I walk past the laundry room, occasionally I stop and have a brief conversation with the staff, especially on a particularly hot day to see how they are doing, to marvel that they can remember which resident gets which clean laundry! (Even with name tags.) When I see one of the maintenance team, I may comment on their work and how important it is to the community. I sometimes talk to the medical team at the nurses' stations or as they are charting in the halls. Seeing both their deep commitment to serve, and the weariness in doing well, I try to be an encourager.

My Commander

rules like a well-marked road
guide and guard
an under-shepherd
to prevent cliff-fall and cast
backbreaking terminus;
rules like order from my Commander,
take the breach, pursue, reach
goal and destiny - never surrender...
      yet, yes, you must surrender
      to the Tender of my soul.
rules like standardized methods
tried and true, true and tried
serving all times, all places
an organic techné that frees
but only as the student trusts, obese,
surrenders.
Rules, the exercise of Authority, Dominion,
      Reign; yet, yes I must surrender
        to Sovereign Rule.

Meditation – Hope

Praying Psalm 128: I reverently fear you, Lord, I follow your ways, you bring joy. Our family is your blessing. I long to see all they do prosper. Grant us peace.

Scripture Text - Romans 8:22-25
But if we hope for what we do not yet have, we wait for it patiently. Romans 8:25

Living in anticipation and expectation can be both exciting and exasperating. We all have vivid memories as a child waiting for something which we desired greatly. For me it was my first bike. I learned to ride a two-wheel bike using my sister's big, heavy, antique, one-speed girl's bike. It was both challenging and embarrassing. I asked my parents repeatedly for a bike of my own, a boy's bike. Then on my eighth birthday I got a beautiful blue, restored, second-hand bike. I was thrilled.

In the months of waiting, which as a seven-year-old seemed like years, I had to be patient.

The Apostle Paul is expounding the majestic theme of hope in Romans 8. Hope in the midst of our suffering, in our waiting, in our fallen, groaning world as we groan in prayer and patient anticipation.

The childhood illustration of waiting for a new bicycle seems trivial and inconsequential compared to the weighty issues we hope for in later life. Hope for an unsaved friend or loved one, hope for a renewed world, hope for the return of Jesus. What are you waiting and hoping for today?

Suggested Song: "My Hope Is Built"

Pray: Heavenly Father, as a trusting and waiting child, I will try to live and pray in such a way that I quietly, confidently, patiently wait in hope for you to work all things according to your good plan. In Jesus' name, Amen.

PRAY AS IF YOUR VERY EXISTENCE DEPENDS ON IT.

Meditation – The Writing on the Wall

✳ **Praying Psalm 129:** Any victories in my life are a direct result of you, O God. May those who oppose you and your truth be turned back, dried up, unfed, unblessed.

📖 **Scripture Text** - Romans 12:9-16
Be joyful in hope, patient in affliction, faithful in prayer. Romans 12:12

Several years ago, we had the verse Romans 12:12 painted by a local sign-maker and artist on a beautiful wall plaque. It hangs in our home.

A life-verse, a "writing on the wall."

This powerful, three-point sermon is simple to remember, but not always so simple to live.

The admonition to be joyful is foundational as we draw our joy from the deep well of living water we find in Jesus. This deep joy gives us hope which strengthens us for the second point: affliction. We are called to suffer for Jesus' sake. We have human afflictions and trials, and we also suffer as we see the fallenness of our world; but we suffer with a resilient patience which comes from God. Through it all, in times of affliction and affirmation, we pray. Persistent, faithful, consistent prayer.

When we forget – we just look up – the writing is on the wall.

🎵 **Suggested Song:**
"What A Friend We Have In Jesus"

🙏 **Pray:** Father, today I ask for help as I choose again to live joyfully in hope, to be patient in this day's affliction, and to continue in joy, hope, and prayer today and the days to come, in Jesus' name, Amen.

Bridge, Ray

Meditation – Endurance

Praying Psalm 130: From the depths of despair, O Lord, I call for your help. Hear my cry. Pay attention to my prayer. You offer forgiveness, assurance, confidence, hope. I placed my hope in you. With you is unfailing love. Your redemption overflows all my disappointments.

Scripture Text - Romans 15:5-6, 13
May the God who gives endurance and encouragement give you the same attitude of mind toward each other that Christ Jesus had. Romans 15:5

During the 1976 Summer Olympics I watched the competitors perform their astounding feats, and for the first time realized the fruit of endurance, if only vicariously. The games were held in Montreal, and as a student I had visited that beautiful city three years earlier, in 1973. Preparations for the big event were already evident in the city. As I watched the games, I felt an affinity and connection to the city, and to the commitment to be faithful to a cause.

As a follower and disciple of Jesus Christ, as he is my Lord and Saviour, I have a much greater cause than running a race in the Olympics (as admirable and inspiring as that feat is). I was inspired to write a little country song that summer with the refrain:
"Now I am running a new race.
It's a race that I'm anxious to run.
The reward is to see my Master's face,
And to hear Him say, 'Well done!'"

Suggested Song: "Great Is Thy Faithfulness"

Pray: Lord, as I follow you today, please give me the endurance to be faithful to you alone, and I give you praise! In Jesus' name, Amen.

I Came to Tabor Court to *Live!*

Esther is a generous person. She loves to bless others in any way she can. She often pays for doughnuts and coffee to bless the staff. She loves to place an envelope into the Chapel offering basket after Sunday service. She is generous in her kindness and encouraging words. She tells friends and family that she came to Tabor Court *"to Live!"* Only her address has changed, not her zest and love of life. Esther is living, loving proof of a person who is generated by generosity. We live – only our address may change.

Irradiation of Revelation

I noticed it first in his face.
His eyes always shone, reflecting
Light of sun and deep earth tones.
Emanating from Source deep within.
While dancing the reflections of children's
Laughter and elders' nod.
But this was different:
Light shone through his face
Forehead blaze, cheekbones shimmer
Jaw and mouth emitting glow from above below.
The top of the head
Irradiation of revelation
Showering out through his clothing
Which no longer was cloth instead
Essential radiance. I could only
Compare it to supernatural bleaching
Leaching from the mountain light.
Dazzling, eye-fission double-vision
Day dawn, Morning Star
Eyewitness to his majesty.
Through light white glory we basked in Pure Love.

Meditation – Love and Loyalty

Praying Psalm 131: Lord, my heart is not proud, my eyes are not haughty. I don't concern myself with matters too great or too awesome for me to grasp. Instead, I have calmed and quieted my soul, like a weaned child who no longer cries for its mother's milk. Yes, like a weaned child is my soul within me.

Scripture Text - Ruth 1:1, 6-7, 16-18
But Ruth replied, "Don't urge me to leave you or to turn back from you. Where you go I will go, and where you stay I will stay. Your people will be my people and your God my God." Ruth 1:16

In adversity and trials, we see a person's true character. Naomi must have been a remarkable woman. For Ruth to have remained loyal and loving to her mother-in-law, even after she had every opportunity to walk away, speaks to the love and loyalty of both women.

Loyalty must be earned. Families need to support and sustain one another. Employers must show care and concern for their employees if they expect company loyalty. Non-profit organizations invest in their staff, donors, and volunteers to the health and benefit of their programs. Churches must be affirming and appreciative of the body of Jesus because our Head lived in a servant-sacrificial way that we are called to follow.

And follow was what Ruth did. She followed Naomi to her homeland, becoming part of a new family, future, and faith. The beautifully moving story of Ruth and Naomi's love and loyalty expanded to bless others in their community and beyond.

Suggested Song:
"I Would Be True"

Pray: Lord Jesus, thank you for being the perfect model of love and loyalty, becoming human and laying down your life for us! We praise you, Amen.

TIME LISTENING TO GOD SPEAK THROUGH HIS WORD IS TIME GLIMPSING ETERNITY.

Meditation – Here I Am

Praying Psalm 132: Lord, remember David and all the greats who sought and planned and worked for your greatness. You are my sanctuary. We are the holy temple you dwell in by the Holy Spirit.

Scripture Text - 1 Samuel 3:1-10
The LORD came and stood there, calling as at the other times, "Samuel! Samuel!" Then Samuel said, "Speak, for your servant is listening." 1 Samuel 3:10

I was admiring the picture on the wall of a cute little six-month-old. The proud great grandma said, "His name is Sammy, named after the prophet Samuel." A big Bible character to emulate! But even the powerful man of God who commissioned kings and challenged churlish characters started out as a child. A responsive child.

"Here I am." Three words that have changed many people's lives. Abraham, Moses, Samuel, and others throughout history. Their willingness to answer the call, to serve faithfully, even fearlessly. The calls continue today. Whether we are named Samuel, Sally, Shirley, or Steven, we are called by the Lord who knows us each by name.

God calls each of us to be in relationship with him. To serve him. We may not be called as a prophet, or a king, but in our unique callings as teachers, construction workers, bakers, lawyers, pastors, doctors, businesspeople, missionaries, and elders, we have the opportunity and the choice to respond, "Here I am. Speak, for your servant is listening."

Suggested Song:
"Here I Am Lord"

Pray: Loving God, I long to serve and follow you today and in the days to come. Speak, Lord, I'm listening. I pray in the powerful name of Jesus, Amen.

Clear View, Marg

Meditation – The Lord is Witness

Praying Psalm 133: I love it, Lord, when we live together in harmony! Shalom -like warm, soothing, healing, anointing oil. Refreshing like mountain dew.

Scripture Text - 1 Samuel 12:1-5
Samuel said to them, "The LORD is witness against you, and also his anointed is witness this day, that you have not found anything in my hand." "He is witness," they said. 1 Samuel 12:5

We used to sing a little children's song, "Be Careful Little Eyes." Some of the lyrics were "Be careful little eyes what you see, for the Father up above is looking down in love, so be careful little eyes what you see." The song then went through our various ways of expressing integrity – ears what you hear, tongue what you say, hands what you do, feet where you go, heart whom you trust, mind what you think. Personal integrity is an essential component to being a disciple of Jesus.

The prophet Samuel was closing down his public ministry. He had lived with integrity and wanted to finish well. He could not be accused of theft, cheating, abuse, oppression, or financial indiscretion (he did not accept bribes). He demonstrated a willingness to make restitution if anyone accused him of wrongdoing. The people replied, "You have not cheated or oppressed us" (verse 4).

What a joyful way to make the transition into his new and next life. He is a good role model for us as we serve and live for God.

Suggested Song: "Be Careful Little Eyes"

Pray: Loving Father, we acknowledge that you witness our lives, may we live pure and blameless lives for your glory and our good, in Jesus' name, Amen.

Sacred Moments

Sharing time, praying, and reading scripture with Annie and her family in her active dying was a privilege. To share the sacred moments of the thin space between earth and heaven. Although Annie was not visibly responsive, we could sense that she was worshipping and praying with us – a great encouragement to her loved ones. The mystery of life and death is great. We have learned much through science and medical advances, we know more about the human body and brain, and yet it is still a wonderful mystery. The honour to enter this quiet room, with the diffuser's gentle aromatic mist, the sound of muted instrumental music, the glistening eyes of loved ones praying silently, is never lost on me. The meeting of heaven and earth. If we only had eyes to see, it is around us at every hour, in every space.

Eyes Wide Open

I keep my eyes open when I pray
Ever since that mountain top day
To catch the glow the glorious ray
I keep my eyes wide open when I pray.

I let my hands fall open to receive
The ounces of glory I perceive
Immeasurable light and linen white
My hands are open to receive.

I stand at the ready to move
In response to awe - gentle shove
Or to turn and run looking above
Watchful and trembling at raw Love.
I stand always ready in prayer to move.

Meditation – Shepherd

Praying Psalm 134: I praise you along with countless others who serve you night and day. We lift our hands towards all that gives you glory. Receiving blessings.

Scripture Text - 2 Samuel 5:1-3

And the LORD said to you, "You will shepherd my people Israel, and you will become their ruler." 2 Samuel 5:2

The role of shepherds in ancient times is a mixed story. On the one hand they were often very poor, mistreated, and ostracized from the upper class. On the other hand, they provided essential services to the community. People love souvlaki. Where would sacrificial lambs come from if there were no shepherds?

David was receiving the commission to become king over Israel. From shepherd to military campaigner to king. God had blessed this Shepherd-King.

Do we ever look down on certain occupations or people as being lowly and unworthy? Are we guilty of class and positional snobbery? God had such high regard for shepherds that they were the first to hear and respond to the glorious angel song at Jesus' birth. Jesus honoured the role of shepherd by calling himself The Good Shepherd, saying *"The good shepherd lays down his life for the sheep."* (John 10:11) The metaphor is meaningful.

We should never despise or reject anyone. They might one day become King.

Suggested Song: "The Lord's My Shepherd"

Pray: Heavenly Father, thank you for sending Jesus to be our Good Shepherd. We pray in his mighty name, Amen.

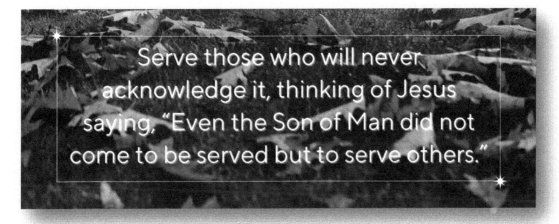

Serve those who will never acknowledge it, thinking of Jesus saying, "Even the Son of Man did not come to be served but to serve others."

Meditation – Let Your Light Shine

Praying Psalm 135: Praise you! Praise your name, Adonai, El Elyona, El Shaddai ... You are good. I celebrate your love, your greatness, for your blessings, and favour. Your will be done, against Pharaohs, Sihon, Og, and all the kings of Canaan. Thank you for safety and your abundant provisions. For your justice and compassion. I join all worship leaders through all time... Praise you!

Scripture Text - 2 Samuel 23:1-4
Like the light of morning at sunrise on a cloudless morning, like the brightness after rain that brings grass from the earth. 2 Samuel 23:4

We lived in a home with a wall of east-facing windows with a peaceful view over a quiet pond. The sunrises were exhilarating. The light of pre-dawn colouring the tree-lined horizon, a sign of promised light to come. The spreading of golden, rosy sky-washed brightness before the full blaze of sunrise was a show worth waking for. In another home we enjoyed looking out on a beautiful green lawn, backed by ornamental grasses. There was a freshness and brightness after a summer rainfall that gave a sense of freshness and life.

Wouldn't you like to be known as a person who brings light and life into the room? What would it be like to see your life contribution as "like the light of morning?" King David in his last words recorded in our passage used both these metaphors to describe his life ministry. Egomaniac? Puffed-up? One would think so if not for one phrase in this text describing the one "anointed by God" (verse 1). In Jesus Christ we are empowered, filled, anointed with the Holy Spirit.
We, like David, are anointed of God.

Let your light shine.

Suggested Song: "This Little Light of Mine"

Pray: Thank you, God, for your anointing power poured out on me through the Holy Spirit. Today help me shine with Father, Son and Holy Spirit, in Jesus' name I pray, Amen

Mossy Woods
BY AMY BERGEN

Meditation – His Banner Over Me Is Love

Praying Psalm 136: Thank you, Lord, you are so good. Your faithfulness endures forever. You alone perform mighty miracles, skilful in creation, faithful in history, remembering our weakness, providing food. You are faithful.

Scripture Text - Song of Songs 2:1-5
Let him lead me to the banquet hall, and let his banner over me be love. Song of Songs 2:4

God is referred to in Exodus 17 as "my Banner" (Yahweh-Nissi). Moses had aided the people of Israel in a crucial battle against the Amalakites. He did so not by flailing a sword or shouting orders to the forces. He aided them by arms uplifted in blessing and intercession (Exodus 17:8-13). To commemorate the prayer-victory event, Moses built an altar and called it The Lord is my Banner (Exodus 17:15).

The singer of love songs in Song of Songs 2 refers to a banner of love. Banners are associated with celebrations (think of a Happy Anniversary or Happy Retirement banner), or with political campaigns and rallies.
Here the banner over the beloved is love.

In one sense this love poem is an expressive, even sensual celebration of human love and sexuality. At a metaphoric level, this poetry has inspired spiritual application. Jesus is our Lover, his banner celebrates his victory over us in love. The setting is a banqueting table. Jesus spoke a lot about weddings and feasts. And we are invited to dine with him. Glory.

Suggested Song: "His Banner Over Me Is Love"

Pray: Loving Saviour, thank you for your banner of love over me today. I enter the banquet hall arm-in-arm with you and join the celebration with thanks, in Jesus' name, Amen.

Bring On Life

It was a lighthearted but significant conversation with Warren about human life expectancy in the Bible. He said, "What is with the 120-year life span? Why aren't we living that long these days?" I asked Warren, who proudly told me he was 80 years old, if he would like to live another forty years. He grinned and said, "For sure!" Long life is a blessing to those who enjoy good health, love, and purpose. Warren is in a wheelchair and sleeps through much of the day, he has a deep faith, a loving family, an enjoyment of scripture, music, and prayer, and he says – bring on life. "Moses was just beginning at my age."

Praying Psalm 137: I long for home. Like being in exile in a foreign land, like Babylon. I weep and I hang my guitar up in the willow branches. I remember home – longing to dwell in the house of the Lord forever. Defend me, protect, release.

Leaving A Legacy

Leaving a legacy, leaving a will
determination to strive on still,
What could be better?
A love, hope, optimism that
even death cannot kill.
Soaring words, "apostolic" charge
fitting for someone who lived life large
now passing the torch
to new leaders and followers
on the path uncharted.
Burst to flame
from your spark
learning from light-giving, life-giving
legacy of energy, vision, determination,
lay down a life, active not latent,
richer and deeper, higher, more patient
a rekindled hope for a nation.

In memory of Jack Layton
(1950-2011)

Meditation – Word of God

Praying Psalm 138: I give you thanks, O Lord, with all my heart. I will sing your praises before the gods (materialism, commercialism, individualism, hedonism...) for your great promises are backed by all the honour of your name. As soon as I pray, you answer me; you encourage me by giving me strength.

Scripture Text - 1 Thessalonians 2:7-13
And we also thank God continually because, when you received the word of God, which you heard from us, you accepted it not as a human word, but as it actually is, the word of God, which is indeed at work in you who believe. 1 Thessalonians 2:13

When we read the Bible, it is unlike any other reading or literary activity. For example, when we read a magazine, it may be for opinions, perspectives, points of view, or maybe we just enjoy the pictures. When we read a novel, we read to enjoy a good story, but we also delight in characters, settings, and expressive language. When we read an instruction manual or a menu, it is for specific directions, decisions, and action.

When we read the Bible, we read it as God's Word. God is speaking. By the Holy Spirit we receive truth, instruction, correction, and encouragement. We read poetry, narrative, history, genealogy, apocalyptic, proverbs, biography (gospel), parables, letters, and each genre needs its own interpretive approach. We read the Bible not only "as a human word," "but as it actually is, the word of God."

When God spoke to prophets, apostles, and faithful followers in the Bible they responded in a variety of different ways. Some fell prostrate on the ground, some questioned or doubted, and some tried to run away.

How will we let God's word work in us today?

Suggested Song: "The B.I.B.L.E."

Pray: Dear God, as I read your word day by day, may I hear your voice in fresh and transforming ways, I pray in Jesus' name, Amen.

— " —
A text without context may become a pretext.
— " —

Meditation – Fruitful Lives

Praying Psalm 139: O Lord, you have examined my heart and know everything about me. Such knowledge is too wonderful for me, too great for me to understand! You knit me together in my mother's womb. I praise you because I am fearfully and wonderfully made. Search me, O God, test me, know me, lead me in the way everlasting.

Scripture Text - 2 Thessalonians 1:3-4, 11-12
With this in mind, we constantly pray for you, that our God may make you worthy of his calling, and that by his power he may bring to fruition your every desire for goodness and your every deed prompted by faith. 2 Thessalonians 1:11

We all want our lives to be fruitful. We have great worth in God's eyes. God created us, gave us talents and personalities that reflect the image of God, we are created for relationship, love, nurture and to bless others.

How wonderful to have someone in our lives to pray for us, as the sisters and brothers in the church of Thessalonica in the first century had Paul praying for them. He prayed they would live in a manner worthy of God's call, that they would see fruits of goodness and faith in their lives. All this comes from God's power.

This is the same power that produces fruit in orchards, vineyards, olive groves all over the world every year. The same power God used to create this beautiful world. The same power that raised Jesus from the dead. The same power that equips the saints for faithfulness and service.

Let us pray for one another for good, fruitful lives.

Suggested Song:
"Make Me A Blessing"

Pray: Father, Son and Holy Spirit, thank you for making me in your image, so I have great worth and potential for a fruitful life. Make me a blessing to someone today, in Jesus' name, Amen.

Blessed, Katy

Praise Him With Dancing

Simi, one of the nurses, loves to dance with residents in Cherry Lane when I play guitar. The rhythm of "This is the Day," or "I've Got the Joy Joy, Joy, Joy Down in My Heart," provides the opportunity to take the hands of Fred or Ralph or Mary and help them stand so they can dance together. Some of them have some good dance moves! Others shuffle their feet and sway side-to-side with a big grin on their face (the way I dance!). The joy and energy of the moment is palpable. I see in those moments a living-out of Psalm 150: *"Praise him with dancing, praise him with the strings. Let everything that has breath praise the LORD."*

Meditation – Eternal Encouragement

Praying Psalm 140: Rescue me, Lord, from evil. Keep me safe from wickedness, from devious, arrogant ways. You are my God, my strong deliverer. You secure justice for the poor and take care of the needy. I live in your presence.

Scripture Text - 2 Thessalonians 2:13-16
May our Lord Jesus Christ himself and God our Father, who loved us and by his grace gave us eternal encouragement and good hope. 2 Thessalonians 2:16

Life can be hard. People make demands on us, maybe our financial picture is dark, health can fail. We need regular encouragement. This encouragement can come in simple ways. As we go through our day, do we make a conscious effort to thank people for their services? Just saying thanks for your help to a store clerk, waiter, receptionist, colleague, can go a long way. Simply being kind to others, treating them as you want to be treated is walking the Jesus way.

How amazing that today's verse uses the superlative "eternal encouragement."

The little lift we receive from an encouraging word is multiplied exponentially, eternally, by *"our Lord Jesus Christ and God our Father who loved us and by his grace gave us eternal encouragement and good hope."*

This eternal encouragement comes from an eternal source, eternally living and moving in the world.

So, when life is hard, remember and live in eternal encouragement and good hope.

Suggested Song: "Leaning on The Everlasting Arms"

Pray: Loving God, I need your eternal encouragement in my life today. As I draw from this endless well of hope, help me share encouragement and kindness to those you bring into my life today. Thank you, in Jesus' name, Amen.

Nebuchadnezzar Dream On

Never giving a second thought to those selected,
Excellent sacred objects won from Jerusalem Temple
Back in Babylon this King gave instructions to keep
Under watchful care the precious objects and youth
Chosen, nurtured, fed on special diet.
Healthy specimens with hard names
Acquired new names, but familiar diet and
Devotion to the God of Israel – these young men –
Nebuchadnezzar's prize – these selected
Excellent sacred objects
Zealous for their God yet sensitive to Babylonian
Zeitgeist, the Spirit of their living God
Arranged for their promotion and protection. These
Rare and valued sacred objects from Jerusalem.

(Daniel 1)

Daniel told his friends to pray
Response from God was on its way
Easy as a dream to say
A bold prediction for the day
Majesty – on feet of clay.　　　　(Daniel 2)

Or, maybe this megalomaniac
Nebuchadnezzar would be a slow learner.

(Daniel 3)

Meditation – Distant Triumph Song

Praying Psalm 141: I call to you, Lord, come quickly to me, hear me when I call you. May my prayer be set before you like incense. Set a guard over my mouth, Lord. Keep watch over the doors of my lips. Do not let my heart be drawn to evil. My eyes are fixed on you, Sovereign.

Scripture Text - 2 Thessalonians 3:1-5
May the Lord direct your hearts into God's love and Christ's perseverance. 2 Thessalonians 3:5

I first heard the hymn "For All the Saints" as a high school choir student. Its soaring melody is named *Sine Nomine* (without name), its majestic choral setting by English composer Ralph Vaughan Williams was thrilling to sing and was always an audience favourite. The lyrics have stayed with me. One phrase is appropriate when we think about perseverance in the faith:
"And when the battle's fierce, the warfare long,
Steals on the ear the distant triumph song.
And hearts are brave again and arms are strong, Alleluia!"
The "distant triumph song" reminds us that Jesus has already won the victory. We still battle against wickedness and evil (verse 2) and there is opposition to the gospel in our world, but the victory is won. When Jesus said on the cross, "It is finished," he was referring to the victory over sin and Satan.
Be encouraged and directed into God's love and Christ's perseverance. And may we be brave and strong for the kingdom.

Suggested Song: "For All the Saints"

Pray: Loving God, thank you for your strength and promise to never leave us. Today, help me to be brave and strong in Jesus' name, Amen.

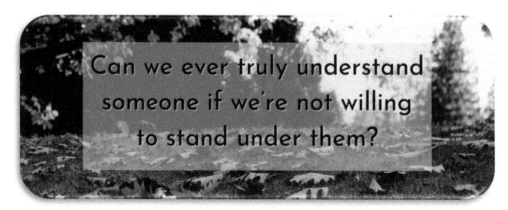
Can we ever truly understand someone if we're not willing to stand under them?

Meditation – In His Mercy

☀ **Praying Psalm 142:** I cry aloud to you, Lord, for mercy. I complain to you, pouring out my troubles. When my spirit grows faint within me you watch over me. You are my refuge, my portion. Set me free from my prison that I may praise your name because of your goodness to me.

📖 **Scripture Text** - 1 Timothy 1:12-17
But for that very reason I was shown mercy so that in me, the worst of sinners, Christ Jesus might display his immense patience as an example for those who would believe in him and receive eternal life. 1 Timothy 1:16

Paul is extremely thankful for God's mercy. Perhaps he reflected on all the times he burst into gatherings of Christians and angrily dispersed them, telling them they were guilty of blasphemy. Maybe he remembered speaking wicked things about the Messianic claims of Jesus. Certainly, the images of Stephen being stoned would have haunted Saul / Paul through his life. (Acts 7:58)

I am extremely thankful for God's mercy. I am amazed at God's patience with me, a sinner, and humbled that God would allow me to serve the kingdom. I came to Christ as a child, I was spared much heartache and harm, for which I thank God. In his mercy, he sheltered and guided my teen and adult life. My testimony, your testimony is different from the apostle Paul's but by God's mercy, he allows each one who believes in Jesus to serve as an example, that others may receive eternal life.

🎵 **Suggested Song:**
"At Calvary"

🙏 **Pray:** Heavenly Father, your mercy is great, your grace is freely poured out on me as I confess my sins, believe in Jesus and receive your eternal life. Thank you, God, in Jesus' name, Amen.

Lagoon, Hudson

Meditation – Entitlement

Praying Psalm 143: Lord, hear my prayer, listen to my cry for mercy; in your faithfulness and righteousness come to my relief. I spread out my hands to you, I thirst for you like a parched land. Your righteousness brings me out of trouble.

Scripture Text - 1 Timothy 6:6-10
But godliness with contentment is great gain. 1 Timothy 6:6

A prevalent attitude in our day is a sense of entitlement. It is as if we are all walking around with a placard sign saying, "You Owe Me!"

Now, living in a free and open society is a wonderful gift, and it includes many rights and privileges. But we need always remember they are privileges given to us as a good gift.

After everything had been stripped away from the epitome of patience and suffering, the character Job in the book bearing his name says, *"Naked I came from my mother's womb, and naked I will depart. The LORD gave and the LORD has taken away; may the name of the LORD be praised."* (Job 1:21)

Paul echoes these words of witness and worship when he says, *"we brought nothing into the world, and we can take nothing out of it"* (verse 7).

The Christian antidote to an unhealthy sense of entitlement is godliness with contentment.

Suggested Song: "Rock of Ages"

Pray: Father God, "nothing in my hands I bring, simply to the cross I cling." Forgive me when I have an attitude of entitlement, for every good gift comes from you, the Father of lights. Thank you, in Jesus' name, Amen.

Join the Journey

"What calendar do you people use in this place?" It was Advent and we had been discussing the concept of anticipation and waiting for the celebration of the first coming of Jesus. We also spoke of the second coming of Jesus. We looked at the Advent Calendar on the wall of the lounge in Willow Lane. Fred asked his question expressing genuine confusion. January to December made sense. Winter – Spring – Summer – Fall, he understood. Fred had been a teacher, so he resonated with the September to June calendar year. But Advent, Christmas, Epiphany, Lent, Easter, Pentecost, were a total mystery to him. "What calendar do you people use?"

Join the journey of the Christian calendar, Fred.

Veiled In Flesh

This vale of tears.
Veiled to be available
To all of us.
Knowing the darkness
Of the valley of death.
As well as the Mount of Transfiguration
Veiling was revealing,
Mocking, spitting.
Could it have failed?
And as his three-decade veil
Was torn by nail and thorn
The veil-barrier to the holiest place
Was ripped open.
Now he has revealed himself
To all of us.
… no longer veiled …
We, the flesh-ones must reveal
As we daily re-veil the Word.

Meditation – Guard It

Praying Psalm 144: Praise you, Lord, my Rock! You train me for spiritual warfare. You are loving and strong, my fortress, shield, and refuge. Who am I that you care for me? I am like a breath, a fleeting shadow. I will sing a new song to you, my God, you protect from the deadly sword of lies – you give victory.

Scripture Text - 2 Timothy 1:11-14

I know whom I have believed and am convinced that he is able to guard what I have entrusted to him until that day. 2 Timothy 1:12

What has God entrusted to you? Not only the many blessings you have received from God, but what specific gifts, talents, and attributes has God allowed you to steward in your life? Maybe it is the ability to encourage others. Maybe it is the gift of faith. Maybe you are a gifted communicator. Maybe you have skills to organize or lead. These are things our Heavenly Father has appointed you to acknowledge, develop and share with others.

Paul acknowledges the gospel – his unique ability to share the good news – as something he was appointed to discharge as a faithful herald, apostle and teacher. He was confident in his call, even though he suffered for it, because of his firm conviction and faith in God's faithfulness. We are stewards of our skills of teaching, singing, praying, and giving, not for our own edification or self-satisfaction, but to invest in God's kingdom. We are to guard these things (verse 14) not jealously, but reverently, and pass them on to our world, all to the glory of God.

Suggested Song:
"I Know Whom I Have Believed"

Pray: Thank you, loving God, for the talents and gifts you have entrusted to me. Help me give them away to others today for their benefit, your glory and my good, I pray in Jesus' name, Amen.

God's Official Community Plan (OCP) provides hope, courage, joy and energy.

Meditation – God-Breathed

Praying Psalm 145: I will exalt you, my God the King. You are great and most worthy to be praised. One generation commends your work to another. You are gracious and compassionate, slow to anger and rich in love.

Scripture Text - 2 Timothy 3:10-17
All Scripture is God-breathed and is useful for teaching, rebuking, correcting and training in righteousness. 2 Timothy 3:16

I taught in a small Christian school in Richmond, B.C., 1980-1984. Sometimes I had to give detentions to my junior high students for some infraction. I tried many different remedial disciplines, including picking up trash, cleaning the chalkboard, tidying the classroom, writing lines like "I will pay attention in class." One day I had what I thought was an inspired method of discipline. I would have them write out 2 Timothy 3:16 twenty or thirty times, depending on the severity of the misdemeanor.

After all, the text says all scripture is good for "rebuking," "correcting," and "training in righteousness." Thankfully, a wise parent took me aside and suggested that using scripture as a punishment was not a good disciplinary method. I think I only assigned it as a punishment a few times. Hopefully, it didn't warp any young minds.

This beautiful text affirms the life-giving, affirming power of all God's Word to provide the path to life "teaching." It also is a guard-rail when we go off-track: "correcting." In an evil world it inspires righteous living: "training." And it is truly God-breathed – life-giving.

Suggested Song: "Thy Word Is a Lamp Unto My Feet"

Pray: Dear God, thank you for the Bible, your holy word to us. It is inspired, breathed-into by you, our living, loving Creator, and it guides us into all truth. Please speak to me today, in Jesus' name, Amen.

Meditation – Reminders

Praying Psalm 146: Praise! I praise you! With all that I am, my whole life, in every song I sing, praise you, my God, even with my dying breath. Powerful people, all mortals will breathe their last and return to dust; they are revered, impressive, influential, but I certainly don't put my trust in them – you are my help. You are the healer, encourager, protector, provider.

Scripture Text- Titus 3:1-8
Remind the people to be subject to rulers and authorities, to be obedient, to be ready to do whatever is good. Titus 3:1

"I already knows more than I does!" This bit of folksy wisdom was shared by a former colleague, a godly senior pastor, when we were driving to a professional development conference. He was joking, but there was a ring of sarcasm in his voice and a twinkle in his eye. We had been discussing the topics of the conference and speculating on some of the "new" ideas for ministry that would be presented. Sometimes we get cynical. He quickly followed this statement up by emphasizing the importance of keeping fresh and growing in our ministry endeavours. We need positive reminders.

Paul encourages Titus to diligently remind the church, because we fall so easily back into ways of foolish disobedience, deception, and inappropriate desires and lifestyles (verses 3-4). We live with the challenge of embodying the truth we know. We remind ourselves every time we spend time reading and studying God's word. We can be inspired by good Christian music and literature, and we need to encourage one another in the faith. Let's remind each other to put it into practice.

Suggested Song: "I Need Thee Every Hour"

Pray: Lord, forgive me for my wayward and disobedient tendencies. Thank you for today's reminder to stay on course, in Jesus' name, Amen.

Each Person Matters

November and early December 2020 had been a devastating time for Tabor Home. COVID-19 had been deadly. Our Mission is to "Care from the heart." As a staff member, your heart is in serving each individual person, and when that person dies, it is heartbreaking. Tabor used an evergreen tree to represent life. On the branches were lights and doves, symbols of hope and peace. Each person matters. They were not statistics or casualties, they have names, loved ones, stories, and each left an impression on us. Our prayer was that this Memory Tree would send its light into December darkness, remembering and celebrating the light each of these people brought into the world. Their memories live on – evergreen.

Rocky Shores, Ursula

Jesus Commended

Turn your eyes upon Jesus
Mystic contemplation
dim distraction of things of earth
      Jesus commended
      the flowers of the field
      and birds in the air.
All of Solomon's projects:
      books, buildings, parks, palaces
cannot compare
      clear, cool air and deep fresh grass
      signs of eternity; signs we will pass.

Turn your eyes upon Jesus.
Building bigger barns
pursuit of ease
only ourselves to please
no thought of greater needs, hunger pleas.
Glory and Grace
seen in The Face
 in the pace of daily humble living
giving thought – time – care

for others, self and God.
An awe-full turning.

Meditation – Small Things

Praying Psalm 147: It is so good to sing praises with sisters and brothers... You are rebuilding your people, bringing us out of captivity; we thank you. We glorify you; we are in awe of you.

Scripture Text - Zechariah 4:5-10
Who dares despise the day of small things? Zechariah 4:10

We live in a culture that is impressed by "bigger, better, bolder." Our consumerism and addiction to novelty is getting us in trouble. We are living beyond our means both personally and globally.

There is a movement that has become somewhat appealing, referred to as minimalism. Other trends towards living more simply and sustainably are catching on. They indicate an attraction to and appreciation for small, simple things. This is countercultural.

The text throws down a challenge: "Who dares despise the day of small things?" God is able to take the small things of this world and do great things. Jesus referred to the kingdom of God being like a tiny seed, he invited children (little ones) to come to him as models of the kingdom, and the Apostle Paul heard God say to him, "My grace is sufficient for you, for my power is made perfect in weakness."

Our weakness, smallness, simplicity is honoured by the Spirit to achieve his purpose.

Suggested Song: "Little Is Much When God is In It"

Pray: Loving Heavenly Father, thank you for taking the small things of this world, the weak things, including me, and using them to your glory, in Jesus' name, Amen.

Winter is a season of hope. Underground, waiting for the right time, spring bulbs are getting ready. Preparing to poke through the hardened soil and create a beautiful, vibrant show of color to lift our spirits. Another word for this optimism is faith.

Meditation – Shout

Praying Psalm 148: Praise you, Lord – all heavens, sky, angels, armies of heaven, sun, moon, stars, clouds, all creatures, we praise you. Kings, rulers, judges, young, old, let's all refocus our true priority. Praise the Lord!

Scripture Text - Zechariah 9:9-13
Rejoice greatly, Daughter Zion! Shout, Daughter Jerusalem! See, your king comes to you, righteous and victorious, lowly and riding on a donkey, on a colt, the foal of a donkey.
Zechariah 9:9

It is most appropriate that this inspiring text is set to glorious music in Handel's *Messiah*. The librettist Charles Jennens wove messianic scripture texts into the lyrics for this timeless oratorio. Every year audiences hear the soaring, jubilant notes of a soprano singing "Rejoice, rejoice greatly. Shout, O daughter of Jerusalem."

The reason to anticipate and celebrate is the transforming message that God will come and live among us. In the context of Zechariah's prophetic prediction, the King is coming! The warfare technology (chariots) and the fear of attack are going to be removed (verse 10). There is the declaration of peace to the nations. So when the angels sang at Jesus' birth "Peace on earth," they echoed and foretold the kingdom and rule of King Jesus.

However, we are always in danger of missing his coming because he doesn't come in a triumphalist way riding in a tank or military parade – he arrives victorious and lowly – so easy to miss.

Suggested Song: "Rejoice the Lord is King"

Pray: Lord, thank you for coming in the person of Jesus Christ as Messiah. I am so glad you have come and that you live in me. In Jesus' name, Amen.

Meditation – My Singing Saviour

☀ **Praying Psalm 149:** I sing a new song to you in the assembly of the faithful. I rejoice in you, my Maker, and Proactive Presence in our day. What a privilege to praise you! May you delight in our praise, we humbly pray.

📖 **Scripture Text** - Zephaniah 3:17-20
The LORD your God is with you, the Mighty Warrior who saves. He will take great delight in you; in his love he will no longer rebuke you, but will rejoice over you with singing. Zephaniah 3:17

I have been a singer all my life. I was born into a musical family. My father had a rich bass voice, played the organ and led choirs in churches. My mother had a lovely soprano voice. I began singing solos in high school, with choirs and with my guitar, as singer-songwriter. Later I studied voice and sang professionally. I have always tried to offer my gift in the service of my loving, singing God.

What a beautiful image in our text of God rejoicing over us "with singing!" The picture is of a loving parent soothing and singing a comforting, calming song. Or it could be a victorious song of rejoicing reminding us of his mighty, saving acts in our life.

One day my singing will stop. My voice will grow weak and fail. I will breathe my last breath and take my Lord's hand as he sings me safely and securely into his eternal presence.

🎵 **Suggested Song:** "He Keeps Me Singing"

⚑ **Pray:** Lord God, I praise you and thank you for saving me and singing over me your song of delight and victory, I receive your gift of eternal life, in Jesus' name, Amen.

Ceasefire

"I feel like it's overdone," he said. "I don't even believe in 'Joy to the World,' it's nonsense." This opened the door for a great conversation. We talked about things he did believe in. We talked about the story of Christmas, the incarnation, about God's love for the world. He listened, asked questions, and still seemed unconvinced. I asked if he had a favourite Christmas song or carol. He thought for a minute. "Silent Night," he eventually said softly. He told the story of the Christmas Eve ceasefire, when soldiers from opposing armies laid down their rifles, sang together, and exchanged small tokens as gifts. Sleep in heavenly peace, Fred.

Praying Psalm 150: Praise the Lord in his holy place, praise him in his mighty heaven. Praise him for his awesome works, praise his unequalled greatness! Praise him with a blast of trumpet and saxophone, praise him with the guitar. Praise him with tambourines and dancing, praise him with strings, flutes, cymbals! Let everything that breathes praise you, Lord.

Sunset, Ray

INDEX OF THEMES

Advent / Christmas 1, 4, 5, 8, 9, 12,

Blessing 24, 31, 32, 37, 86, 96, 116, 118, 126, 132, 140, 158, 160

Care 28, 42, 59, 62, 69, 80, 83, 108, 109

Change 2, 3, 14, 15, 16, 33, 34, 36, 48, 54, 56, 57, 64, 74, 87, 102, 105, 119, 121, 122, 125, 126, 133, 139, 141, 148, 162, 165, 172, 180, 189,

Church 51, 63, 74, 75, 103, 122, 123, 140, 143, 146, 153, 188, 191

Creation / New Creation 2, 3, 6, 14, 15, 38, 56, 65, 68, 71, 87, 115, 158, 160, 168, 178, 180

Death 29, 51, 78, 145, 154 157, 158, 159, 163, 168, 185, 193, 199, 211

Discipleship 2, 4, 5, 6, 12, 14, 15, 21, 26, 32, 66, 71, 83, 89, 119, 123, 131, 136, 144, 150, 152, 160, 162, 166, 170, 171, 172, 186, 189, 192

Easter / Palm Sunday 55, 60, 70, 79, 84, 88, 108, 109, 146, 159, 206

Epiphany 17, 21, 25

Faith 6, 34, 35, 38, 44, 65, 66, 68, 71, 76, 80, 81, 86, 89, 91, 93, 95, 98, 102, 109, 114, 119, 126, 133, 140, 170, 175, 185, 189,

Giving 10, 41, 109, 135, 158, 196

Grace 35, 41, 47, 51, 56, 58, 67, 95, 107, 116, 127, 129, 139, 141, 145, 176, 180, 202, 221

Growth 7, 41, 47 ,61 ,67, 109, 116, 122, 128, 145, 155, 156, 160, 166, 181, 183, 188, 189, 192

Humility 12, 26, 35, 40, 58, 98, 161, 168, 196,

Hope 1, 44, 71, 72, 75, 81, 86, 93, 94, 124, 126, 139, 153, 158, 167, 167, 173, 176, 177, 185, 187, 188, 199, 202, 211,

Joy 1, 5, 14, 51, 56, 90, 98, 104, 154, 167, 181, 183, 188, 202

Love 4, 5, 7, 14, 28, 35, 38, 40, 41, 42, 44, 60, 74, 77, 80, 83, 89, 90, 91, 95, 107, 109, 118, 120, 129, 144, 145, 148, 173, 175, 180, 181, 185, 190, 191, 194, 198, 199, 201, 216

Music 4, 32, 36, 39, 47, 95, 116, 120, 154, 174, 184, 193, 198, 210, 214, 215

Obedience 18, 50, 80, 102, 106, 115, 135, 143, 156, 171, 183, 189, 191, 210,

Peace 8, 31, 32, 38, 58 ,84, 88, 93, 130, 133, 139, 170, 196, 211, 214, 216

Prayer 4, 5, 8, 16, 21, 34, 36, 38, 40, 41, 43, 48, 58, 59, 68, 87, 102, 114, 118, 122, 130, 136, 141, 146, 152, 163, 170, 177, 186, 194, 198

INDEX OF BIBLE TEXTS

Ray Harris is a follower of Jesus, a husband, father, and Papa to their eight grandchildren. Ray loves providing spiritual care for older adults, singing with them, reading God's word together, and coming alongside those in their journey with Jesus who need encouragement and prayer. He is a pastor, teacher, musician, a reader and writer.
He lives in Abbotsford BC and enjoys walking along Horn Creek Trail.
He holds graduate degrees in music and Christian studies.

Printed in the USA
CPSIA information can be obtained
at www.ICGtesting.com
JSHW040229051123
51245JS00003B/4